W9-BEQ-175

STORIES
BEHIND THE
GREATEST HITS
of
CHRISTMAS

ACE COLLINS

ZONDERVAN®

ZONDERVAN.com/
AUTHOR**TRACKER**
follow your favorite authors

ZONDERVAN

Stories Behind the Greatest Hits of Christmas
Copyright © 2010 by Andrew Collins

This title is also available as a Zondervan ebook. Visit www.zondervan.com/ebooks.

This title is also available in a Zondervan audio edition. Visit www.zondervan.fm.

Requests for information should be addressed to:

Zondervan, *Grand Rapids, Michigan 49530*

Library of Congress Cataloging-in-Publication Data

Collins, Ace.
    Stories behind the greatest hits of Christmas / Ace Collins.
      p.   cm.
    ISBN 978-0-310-32795-0 (hardcover, jacketed)
   1. Carols—History and criticism. 2. Christmas music—History and
criticism. 3. Popular music—United States—History and criticism. I. Title.
ML2880.C65 2010
 782.42'1723—dc22   2010024266

Published in association with Hartline Literary Agency, Pittsburgh, Pennsylvania 15235.

Cover design: Jeff Gifford
Cover photography: Veer®
Interior design: Michelle Espinoza

Printed in the United States of America

10 11 12 13 14 /DCI/ 21 20 19 18 17 16 15 14 13 12 11 10 9 8 7 6 5 4 3 2 1

STORIES
BEHIND THE
GREATEST HITS
of
CHRISTMAS

Other Books by Ace Collins

To Brenda Lee,
for all the joy she has given
through her records and stage performances

Contents

CHRISTMAS HITS

et ready to be surprised by Christmas songs!

Did you know it was a Christmas song that introduced the world to modern electronic recording? Did you have any idea that many of the greatest hits of the season were penned by Jewish songwriters? Have you ever considered how many Christmas hits do not contain a single reference to the holiday? Did you have a clue that it was a famous Christmas song that all but ruined a budding country music star's career?

Christmas songs never really leave us. Just like clockwork, they annually come back to set the holiday mood. They are less like old songs and more like familiar friends—just like the folks who sing them. Consider that without these holiday hits, entertainers like Bing Crosby and Perry Como may have faded and their songs been buried in another era. Yet now they come back to us each year with the regularity of Santa himself and make our holidays sing.

A few special Christmas songs are like time machines: just hearing a few notes from our favorite holiday tunes can magically transport us to a cherished moment from our past.

In this book, thirty-four all-time great Christmas songs are arranged in almost chronological order according to when they hit the charts, with the exception that the first has been moved to last, to honor "Silent Night" as not just the first hit holiday recording but also the most performed Christmas song in history. Each chapter is written with the goal of making the music of the season an even more welcome annual visitor to your home and to your heart by presenting the places and the people behind them in a fresh light and by providing details you likely didn't know about these wonderful musical Christmas cards.

As it says in one of the popular holiday carols covered in these pages, there's no place like home for the holidays, and nothing takes us home like Christmas music. The musical numbers in this book are the ones the public chose as favorites. They are the songs that made the greatest impact by touching hearts and minds in a special way. From among the thousands of Christmas songs written and recorded, these are the holiday hits, and the stories behind them!

O COME, ALL YE FAITHFUL

deste Fideles," better known in America as "O
Come, All Ye Faithful," is a beloved religious carol
that owes its existence to a conflict between religious denominations. On March 31, 1925, Columbia Records
invited participants of a convention held by the Associated Glee Clubs of America to perform at the Metropolitan
Opera House in New York City. Nearly five thousand men
responded. Not only were they asked to perform a dynamic
arrangement of "O Come, All Ye Faithful" beamed live via
radio to a nation, but also their appearance at the grand old
hall was trumpeted as the largest choral performance ever
recorded and placed on a record.

Why did Columbia pick the Associated Glee Club of
America, an amateur group, to earn this honor? It was all
about hype. The glee club movement had all but consumed
the amateur musical scene. Every community of any size
had at least one of these singing groups. The national con-
ventions drew thousands. Those thousands would buy the
recording to show off to their family and neighbors, who in

turn would likely purchase it because they knew someone on it. Hence there was an interested consumer base numbering in the tens of thousands before the record was even produced.

The recording giant was also using the Glee Club's concert as a way of promoting its new electrical recording process, which employed a microphone rather than an acoustic recording horn. The company believed that the recordings would signal such a dramatic improvement in sound quality that the results would awe audiences and thus radically improve its bottom line. Columbia's executives claimed that this new technology would produce a record that was so lifelike, fans could actually feel as if they were there as the record was being recorded. It was like moving from analog to high definition in the world of television. Assembling the world's largest choir seemed the perfect way to showcase the potential of this electronic marvel.

Columbia wanted to use a Christmas song in this unique recording session. Along with "Silent Night," "O Little Town of Bethlehem," and "Joy to the World," "O Come, All Ye Faithful" was one of America's favorite sacred holiday carols. Record executives believed that of the four, "O Come, All Ye Faithful" was the best song to spotlight the potential of electronic recording, and the only one that could be arranged to take advantage of having hundreds of strong male voices on a stage and many more singing from the audience.

The audio equipment needed to produce this immense recording venture was developed in the laboratories of

Western Electric. Columbia brought the men responsible for creating the innovation to New York. That team spent more than a week setting up and testing recordings made from the Metropolitan Opera's grand stage — a painstaking process that involved having small choirs sing from various spots on the stage, listening to those test recordings, then moving the microphones and adjusting equipment as they tested other areas. Scores of test recordings were made in an attempt to capture uniform sound from every spot in the hall. The technicians were still making adjustments just minutes before the performance of the combined glee clubs.

To maximize the effectiveness of the event, Columbia offered the concert for broadcast to the new medium of radio. As stations jumped on board, the company had ready-made publicity for the record they would release if the event proved successful.

Columbia was also taking advantage of a national craze that centered on men joining local singing groups and choruses. Glee clubs were the rage, and an all-star glee club created buzz in almost every community in the nation. Millions were eager to hear the concert.

The sound that came forth that evening left the audience members in such awe that few had words to describe the power and majesty of the group's combined talents. Though the project was considered experimental, the sound was uniform, the mix perfect, the harmonies clear, and the scale of the recording was beyond what most could imagine. Even by modern standards, the quality of the recording is still an example of outstanding production work. With the old-fashioned "horn" method of recording, this monumental feat simply couldn't have been accomplished.

The version of "O Come, All Ye Faithful" recorded by the Associated Glee Clubs of America was probably meant for a holiday release. With widespread newspaper and radio coverage of the recording session, Columbia opted to strike while the iron was hot. The holiday classic was shipped to stores in June 1925. The label proudly carried the news that this was a "WE" recording, meaning the record had been made using Western Electric's microphone system.

Much as with widely anticipated releases of today, such as the first album by *Britain's Got Talent* sensation Susan Boyle, fans rushed to stores to buy the record. Even in the midst of Independence Day parades, radio stations played the release, bringing the Christmas spirit to listeners as fireworks lit up the night skies. Within weeks, this recording had become the best-selling Christmas record in history.

This was not the first time "O Come, All Ye Faithful" had made a trip up the charts, but the new version proved to be a monster hit. Sales stayed hot into the winter as it became the most listened-to holiday record during that Christmas season, and it continued selling during the holidays and well into the next decade.

Sales proved that Columbia made the right choice from among the four holiday classics. Scores of critics echoed this fact as they declared this recording the best in history. But where had this song come from?

For years it was thought that St. Bonaventure had written the lyrics to "O Come, All Ye Faithful" and that a British composer had penned the music. Many in the 1920s audiences listening to Columbia's best-selling recording also thought this was true. Some radio announcers even declared that the song was a thousand years old. It came as quite a shock when, two decades after the introduction of the electronic recording of "O Come, All Ye Faithful," English scholar Maurice Frost discovered seven transcripts of the carol that were written by hand and signed by an English Catholic priest, John Francis Wade. Why had so many been mistaken about the authorship of this great song? That story may well have been the result of religious discrimination.

In 1745, at the age of thirty-five, John Francis Wade found that his life was in grave danger. A cultural war had broken out between the Church of England and the Roman Catholic Church. In England, the Catholic faith was forced underground. As a priest, Wade was sought by the law and bore a price on his head. He secretly crossed the English Channel to France and joined hundreds of other English Catholic refugees who feared they would never be allowed to return to their native land to practice their faith.

In addition to being a cleric, Wade was a calligrapher and a skilled musician. The exiled priest assumed the role of translating and preserving ancient church music. He distributed his work to churches throughout Europe, and some pieces were smuggled back to England. Through his manuscripts, the priest reintroduced many forgotten songs to congregations all across Europe.

Inspired by the centuries-old pieces he was studying, Wade took up pen and, using the style and Latin language of the ancient church, created several new songs that complemented those he had researched. His "Adeste Fideles (O Come, All Ye Faithful)" was published twice in France in the decade after he took up residence there. In both cases, authorship was assigned to Wade. Perhaps because of the Catholic priest's status as a leader in the English Catholic revolution and his refusal to take an oath of allegiance to the Church of England, Wade's name was deleted when Frederick Oakeley translated the original lyrics into English in 1841. Soon St. Bonaventure was given credit for the words and music to "O Come, All Ye Faithful." Even in that guise, the song did not become a popular standard in Britain for another one hundred and twenty years.

In 1860, "O Come, All Ye Faithful" was performed in the Portuguese Embassy in London. After the performance, the organist, Vincent Novello, told members of the press that John Redding had composed the melody. Redding jumped in and took credit for "O Come, All Ye Faithful" and published it under his name. With its new English translation and mass release in print, the song really took off. Within a generation, the carol was the most popular English choral anthem during the holiday season and was enjoyed by carolers all over the world.

Years later, the Peerless Quartet was the most commercially successful vocal group of the acoustic recording era. It would not be an exaggeration to say that the members of the Peerless Quartet were the Beatles of their time. In 1905, this *a capella* group cut "O Come, All Ye Faithful," and it climbed into the seventh spot on America's charts during the week of Christmas.

The Peerless Quartet's cover of the song would remain a holiday standard until 1915. In that year, the world's most famous Irish tenor, John McCormack, took "O Come, All Ye Faithful" to second place on the hit parade. A decade later came the musical revolution led by the Associated Glee Clubs of America. Another decade passed before the voice that came to define holiday music put its spin on Wade's classic carol.

Though it was used as a B-side, Bing Crosby's version of "O Come, All Ye Faithful" gained so much radio play in the 1930s and 1940s that many assumed it had charted a half-dozen times. This is the version of the Christmas classic that is best remembered today. It was during the time when Bing's voice was often heard singing "O Come, All Ye Faithful" that music historian Maurice Frost finally discovered that John Wade should get the credit for his song after centuries of anonymity.

"O Come, All Ye Faithful" was created because of a religious revolution. In the midst of that cultural and theological war between two powerful branches of the Christian faith, a priest who had fled his homeland, fearing for his life, composed a song that almost two hundred years later helped to usher in a new way of producing music. Having since been recorded by thousands more using the "electronic microphone," and now being recorded digitally today, "O Come, All Ye Faithful" retains its charismatic and majestic power and its deep spiritual message, and continues its reign as one of the holiday's greatest hits.

2

JINGLE BELLS

*F*or a century and a half, "Jingle Bells" has defined Christmas for millions of people around the globe. The song's infectious lyrics create the imagery of the holiday season in such vivid detail that artists, tunesmiths, and writers have used the song as inspiration for everything from Christmas cards to hit records to movie sets and Broadway plays. Without "Jingle Bells," there would be no "Jingle Bell Rock" or the famous sleigh ride scenes in films such as *Holiday Inn* or *Christmas in Connecticut*. "Jingle Bells" created the iconic American image of Christmas, an image now treasured around the world.

Ironically, the song was not even written about the Christmas season. When you examine the lyrics of this famous carol, you'll note there's not a single reference to Christmas — not a mention of Santa, Jesus, gifts, trees, or carols and only a nod to Fanny Bright and a bobtailed steed. In fact, this ditty actually examines the dating rituals of teenagers during the cold Northeastern winters in the nineteenth century. The song is about wowing pretty girls by racing horse-drawn sleds. How did this song inspire the likes of Currier and Ives to create a Christmas filled with sleighs and jingling bells? Like much of life, it was all about timing.

In 1840, James S. Pierpont was a young man with too much time on his hands. At least that was his father's perspective. The elder Pierpont, the pastor of the Unitarian church in Medford, Massachusetts, sent his son on errands and assignments at every opportunity. One year, James was assigned to direct the church's adult and children's choirs. James was a gifted musician who knew his way around the piano and the organ and was a vocalist whose voice knew no rival in the small New England community. The young man was the perfect choice for a church choirmaster. Though his work was appreciated in Medford, few realized that James would ultimately change the celebration of Christmas.

James was asked by his father to create a song for a special thanksgiving service at the church. Technically, Thanksgiving was not an official American holiday, but many towns in the country annually set aside special days to count their blessings as the Pilgrims had soon after landing on the shores of the New World. For years, Medford's citizens had celebrated with food, fellowship, and song. Pastor Pierpont was probably expecting James to write lyrics that embraced a theme of "thanks" and incorporated the historic nature of the holiday. James may have planned to do just that, but events outside the family home at 87 Mystic Lane inspired a different type of song.

Suffering from writer's block, James looked out the front window of the Pierponts' house. He saw young men sledding on a snow-covered hill. Bundling up, he stepped outside, where he not only watched but also, caught up in the moment, began to cheer on the participants. For at least an hour, he became a part of the action, riding down the hill a few times on a borrowed sled. By the time the afternoon activities had wound down, he was cold, but as giddy as a child.

As he stepped back into his home and dusted the snow from his clothes, he recalled racing horse-drawn sleds against other boys when he was a teen. He laughed as he remembered the way the girls embraced the winner of those races. He had won a few himself and received hugs for his efforts. Now, that was something to be thankful for! Inspired, he sat down by the fire and started a poem about those experiences. Within minutes, he had composed a few rough verses and added a simple melody. To finish the song, James needed a piano. Throwing on his wet coat, the preacher's son struggled through the deep snow to the home of Mrs. Otis Waterman, who owned the only piano in Medford. When the woman answered the door, James announced, "I have a little tune in my head." She was so familiar with James and his habits that she invited him in.

James later told newspapers that as he sat down at the keys and let his fingers work out the melody, Mrs. Waterman listened and noted, "That is a merry little jingle you have there." When he finished an hour later, the woman assured

James that this song was something the townsfolk would love. Later that evening, he rewrote his lyrics, combining Mrs. Waterman's "jingle" with his observations of that day's sled races and his memories of racing horse-drawn sleighs. He shared the work with his father.

The preacher must have had a great sense of humor, because he allowed James to teach his "One Horse Open Sleigh" to the children's choir at the Medford church. The fully harmonized and whimsical song made its debut at the annual Thanksgiving service in front of a packed house. This song about horse racing and dating was so well received by the congregation that many left humming the tune. Over the course of the next few weeks, scores of members, who couldn't get the melody out of their heads, asked if the choir could sing it again. The elder Pierpont instructed his son to have the choir perform "One Horse Open Sleigh" during the services on Christmas weekend. That performance changed the nature, look, and feel of an American Christmas.

Many visitors from Boston and New York arrived in Medford to visit family and were in the church when James and his choir sang his song for a second time. Because of the timing of "One Horse Open Sleigh," they assumed it was a new Christmas song. Many were so charmed by the simple number that they even learned the melody and wrote down the lyrics. A few of them shared the holiday ditty with those in their own communities. The association of "Jingle Bells" with Christmas started to spread across the New England landscape.

James Pierpont had no idea of the infectious power of his jingle. He only knew that folks in Medford seemed to like his winter song. A few years later, when he moved to Savannah, Georgia, he took his musical one-horse open sleigh with him. Most in the South had never seen a one-horse sleigh, but they responded to the song. James found a publisher for "One Horse Open Sleigh" in 1857. The timing couldn't have been better, as Christmas celebrations were finally becoming a part of the American culture. But it was not until the *Salem Massachusetts Evening News* did a story on the carol in 1864 that the song really caught on. By 1870, "Jingle Bells" was the most popular American Christmas carol. Sheet music sales of James's song caused cash registers to jingle in every state in the union and placed jingling coins in Pierpont's pockets. The song was popular in the American caroling movement that was sweeping the nation in the 1870s and 1880s.

However, it wasn't until the Great Depression that the holiday song became a hit recording. More than seventy years after "Jingle Bells" was written, a ten-year-old Benny Goodman picked up a clarinet. Within six years he was recognized as one of the Windy City's most creative and talented musicians and was asked to join Ben Pollack's California-based band.

Twenty-five-year-old Goodman was in New York when he formed his own group in 1934. Within six months, the Benny Goodman Orchestra had a Saturday night radio show on NBC called *Let's Dance*. Goodman was playing a new sound called swing. The music didn't catch on at first. The band almost starved until a group of teens caught Goodman's act at Palomar Ballroom in Los Angeles. Within months, America's teenagers put the group on the map and jump-started a career that landed Goodman on the *Billboard* charts 164 times.

As the band's fame skyrocketed, Goodman cut an instrumental swing version of "Jingle Bells" that became the biggest Christmas hit of the year. In 1941, another big-band icon, Glen Miller and His Orchestra, recut "Jingle Bells" and moved the holiday classic to number 5 on the charts. This marked the first time Pierpont's lyrics (though rewritten a bit for a modern age) had been employed on a hit recording. During World War II, Bing Crosby pulled the sensational Andrews Sisters into a recording studio to put their spin on "Jingle Bells." Bing's easygoing style combined with the jump-jive rhythms of Maxene, Patty, and LaVerne made for a record that embraced the spirit of fun and play that Pierpont had captured on that day more than a century before. The number also promoted an upbeat message needed during a time when the entire world was at war. This version, still annually played in every corner of the globe, charted in 1943 and again in 1947 and became a jukebox hit for decades.

Today, "Jingle Bells" is one of the first Christmas carols most children learn. People hang jingle bells on their doors, buy wrapping paper and greeting cards featuring one-horse sleighs, and hum the song throughout the holiday season. This uniquely American classic has changed the face of the Christmas season, but no one seems to recall that the song composed on Mystic Lane was really meant for Thanksgiving!

3

WINTER WONDERLAND

"Winter Wonderland" may be the only holiday song that owes its magical, upbeat lyrics to a devastating terminal disease. Had not a young man been struck by tuberculosis, this popular anthem to the season of snow might never have been written.

Dick Smith was in his early thirties and battling tuberculosis, but after years of fighting, he was tired of the struggle. Weak and in pain, Smith spent most of his time in bed, with no hope for a cure. He seemed to be waiting to die.

Smith was a songwriter by trade. He specialized in supplying lyrics for those who created music, but he had yet to score a hit. Because of coughing fits that left him gasping for oxygen, he could barely sit up, much less write. On a depressing, cold afternoon in 1934, Smith pulled himself out of his bed in the West Mountain Sanitarium. He had come to Scranton, Pennsylvania, ostensibly for treatment for his TB, but in his heart he knew he had come there to die.

Looking out the window at the city park, he noticed a half-dozen children playing in the snow. They didn't have a care in the world. Cracking the window open, Smith listened to the kids' voices. He watched them organize a snowball fight. He watched them team up to build a snowman. He grinned as they talked to the snowman as if he were real and danced around the frozen figure.

The songwriter wanted to go out and join them. He longed to play one more time in the snow, but his thirty-three-year-old body was far too weak, his lungs incapable of drawing enough air. For more than an hour, he lived vicariously through the children.

With the sunlight fading, Smith watched the children head home. Then he struggled back across the room to a table. He picked up a pencil and jotted down his thoughts. For a few moments, he felt young, healthy, and strong. While his mind momentarily brought him back to life, his body quickly unmasked the charade, as simply moving the pencil became a monumental task.

Over the next few hours, Smith created a poem about enjoying the wonders of winter. His verses were a blend of the activities he had watched and his own memories. He injected a brief ode to young love. Rereading the lines, he was sure he had just created his best work. He no longer wanted to die. Now he had something to live for!

His poem became a tonic. Smith recovered enough to leave this treatment facility. He took his lyrics to Felix Bernard, a professional pianist who also composed music. More than a writing partner, he was also Smith's friend. The darkness that Bernard usually saw in Smith's eyes was gone.

Energy flooded his voice. As the pianist read the poem, he understood the source of life and joy. Bernard knew that, if coupled with the right melody, the song might attract the interest of a major performer.

Bernard married Smith's lyrics to an upbeat tune. Satisfied they had created something special, the men then began to shop their latest work. Getting "Winter Wonderland" recorded gave Smith a new lease on life. This was more than just a song; it was his legacy. Bernard felt the time pressure in finding the right recording artist, because he knew that if the song wasn't recorded soon, Smith wouldn't see the fruit of his labors. Bernard wanted to give his friend the satisfaction of having a hit song.

"Winter Wonderland" circulated throughout the publishing community during the late spring and early summer of 1934. No one jumped on it. The song might have been lost altogether if Joey Nash, lead singer of the Richard Himber Orchestra, hadn't found a copy of it. After a single reading, the vocalist sensed its potential and took "Winter Wonderland" to his boss.

Initially it appeared that Nash had found "Winter Wonderland" too late. Himber had already gathered enough songs for their next recording session. But at the session, Nash suggested they give "Winter Wonderland" a try. The band rushed through the song before the next group needed the studio. RCA chose to release the song a few weeks later.

When Guy Lombardo listened to the new recording, he was taken back to his childhood. Lombardo couldn't get the song out of his head. Something about "Winter Wonderland" haunted him throughout the night. Rushing into the studio, the bandleader cut his own version with his Royal Canadians. This recording was released by Decca Records.

As Lombardo had already earned more than seventy chart singles, including many number 1 hits, radio stations and stores naturally picked his recording over that by the unproven Himber. Released in early December, Lombardo's version of "Winter Wonderland" raced up the charts, falling one spot short of becoming the groups' twelfth number 1 record.

As Dick Smith listened to Lombardo's version of his song on the radio, he sensed that something special had happened. He'd created a few lines that gave him a brush with fame and success. In those lyrics was his youth. In that sense, even as illness consumed him, he was forever young. In a unique way, he had been given immortality. As long as even one person listened to or sang "Winter Wonderland," a part of Smith would remain on earth, healthy and happy.

"Winter Wonderland" became a hit again in 1935, this time for Ted Weems, but Dick Smith never heard it. He died in the fall, months before winter snows again covered the grounds of the park in his hometown. Lombardo's version of "Winter Wonderland" would be the last Smith would know.

By World War II, more than twenty acts had cut "Winter Wonderland." During the war, Perry Como and the Andrews Sisters put their stamp on the song. In 1947, Johnny Mercer raced up the charts with it. In the slang of the time, "the song had legs."

In the 1950s, a second version of the lyrics to "Winter Wonderland" was created. When Smith wrote the original, he had the kids name the snowman Parson Brown. At that time, most people realized that "parson" is the title for a Protestant minister, but for the new generation, the term was all but unknown. Many felt it was Mr. Brown's first name, and the lyrics were adapted to address this problem. In this version, the verse no longer spoke of a couple being married by a snowman; instead the snowman was a circus clown. Smith's ode to young love was removed from "Winter Wonderland."

By the 1960s, however, most who recorded the song switched back to Smith's original lyric lines, and the wedding scene returned to the song. No matter which version was used, "Winter Wonderland" retained its universal appeal. This was proven as it was recorded by artists as varied as Tony Bennett, Rosemary Clooney, Elvis Presley, and Frank Sinatra. As the years passed, Bob Dylan, Cyndi Lauper, Ozzy Osbourne, and Dolly Parton added their vocal stamps to the number.

On those dismal days when Dick Smith faced his own mortality in a small, sterile room, children playing outside his window brought him the tonic he needed to once more embrace life. Buoyed by the happiness and wonder in the voices he heard that day, he penned one of the most upbeat songs ever to grace the musical world. A man whose short life was filled with pain and suffering is now remembered as the creator of a magical look at the joy to be found on a carefree winter's day.

SANTA CLAUS IS
COMING TO TOWN

*I*n the midst of great personal pain, an old memory of a mother's warning produced the basis for one of the Christmas holiday's most unique hits. More akin to a Tim Burton film than to anything Frank Capra ever produced, "Santa Claus Is Coming to Town" is filled with both the rich anticipated joy of the season and a deep sense of dread. In the world of Christmas music, there is nothing like it.

Covington, Kentucky, was not an easy place to make a living. The rural hills overlooking the Ohio River hid large pockets of poverty. In 1888, James Lamont Gillespie was born into a family that was just scraping by on grit alone. The family of eleven lived in a tiny, dirty, rodent-infested basement apartment. Though he was bright and inquisitive, desperate situations at home forced James, now called Haven, to drop out of school to find work. He struggled, doing odd jobs, until he moved to Chicago and began work as a typesetter.

Gillespie called the Windy City home until he was twenty,

when he returned to Covington to marry and take a job for a local newspaper. In his spare time, he entertained vaudeville audiences with his original jokes and songs. The lure of the stage grew so strong that Gillespie gave up his day job for the spotlight.

His first big break in show business came in 1911, when he joined a dance act and created a show that spotlighted songs he had penned. Local sales of sheet music encouraged him to devote his spare time to composing.

In 1925, Gillespie finally scored a major hit with a song called "Drifting and Dreaming," recorded by George Olson. Yet the songs Gillespie penned afterward failed to catch on. He was forced to turn to newspaper reporting for the *New York Times*. Even as he covered the big-city beat, he kept trying to place his songs with artists and publishers.

At the same time that Gillespie was pitching tunes and scribbling news stories, a nationally known radio star was looking for a new Christmas song. Eddie Cantor, born Edward Israel Iskowitz in New York City, the son of Russian-Jewish immigrants, was orphaned before his second birthday. At the age of fifteen, he was a minor act in vaudeville. Through sheer determination, he worked his way to a top-billed act and caught the eye of the Ziegfeld Follies in 1917. By 1929, he was a star on both coasts, had a string of hit records, and was the toast of Broadway. Then the stock market crash wiped him out.

Yet Cantor bounced back. His dynamic, machine-gun-paced comedy routines and humorous, self-penned songs were perfect for both film and the airwaves. By 1933, he was the world's highest-paid radio star and a top box office draw. Cantor understood the power of public relations. As he looked at the plight the Depression had created for millions, he sensed the need for a bright holiday song. For months, Cantor tried to write his own Christmas lyrics, but he could never create anything that really grabbed him. The performer began calling publishers to see if they had anything they could pitch to him. Leo Feist told Cantor he had something that just needed a bit of tweaking. He'd have it on his desk in a week. Feist was lying. He didn't have a holiday song in his files. But he did know a newspaper reporter who had a knack for creating funny, upbeat lyrics.

When Gillespie got the call, he was in shock. He had just received the news that his brother had died in Kentucky. He initially refused to meet with Feist, but his need for money pushed him to lay his grief aside and make the trip across town to the publisher's office. When Gillespie heard what Feist wanted, he shook his head, informing the man he was not in the mood to spin a yarn filled with hope.

Feist refused to give up. He begged Gillespie to try to create something for Cantor. However, the songwriter left the publisher's office and boarded the subway, determined to focus on his great loss rather than on his craft. Ultimately, the memories flooding his soul became the inspiration for the song Feist wanted and Cantor needed.

When Gillespie was a child, his mother often reminded each of her children that Santa not only knew when they were sleeping but also knew when they were good or bad. Gillespie must have grinned as he thought of the way his mother's warnings had caused all of the kids to toe the line around the holidays. Removing an envelope from his coat pocket as he sat in the train, the writer began to jot down the images filling his head. He envisioned his late brother's reaction as his mother pointed her finger at him and said, "You better watch out, you better be good, because Santa Claus is soon coming to town."

Like many songwriters, Gillespie framed his thoughts in poetry. In the span of fifteen minutes, he penned verses that brought his memories of a childhood, his mother, and his brother to life. By the time he arrived at his stop, he had accomplished what Feist wanted. With the new lyrics in hand, Gillespie sought his friend and music composer John Coots.

As he studied the poem, Coots discovered that the words had a clickety-clack rhythm like the train Gillespie was riding as he wrote the lyrics. The musician latched onto the concept and went to work at the piano. Within twenty-four hours, he presented it to Feist. The publisher rushed it over to the entertainer who needed a holiday hit.

Cantor had rejected scores of new compositions by the time he reviewed "Santa Claus Is Coming to Town." But he instantly knew this song was something special. Two months later, he introduced "Santa Claus Is Coming to Town" on a nationwide broadcast from the Macy's Thanksgiving Day Parade. Cantor was so sure the song would become a hit that he had already had his label, Melotone Records, press the record and ship it to stores. Working with the publisher, Cantor printed the sheet music and shipped it to stores across the nation. Within twenty-four hours of its radio debut, "Santa Claus Is Coming to Town" had sold more than thirty thousand records and a hundred thousand copies of sheet music.

While it seemed the whole world was smiling at the holiday ditty, one man cried every time he heard it. Haven Gillespie always associated the song with his brother's death. Although it brought him more royalties than anything else he ever wrote, he tried to avoid listening to "Santa Claus Is Coming to Town." Scores of artists jumped in line to record it, and Gillespie would never be able to escape the song or the memories it conjured up.

When the song was released, few noted the subtle message created by "Santa Claus Is Coming to Town." They saw the holiday offering as little more than a morality play set to music. Some even latched onto it as a new take on the Golden Rule and as a wonderful way to keep their kids in line.

As the years passed, however, a new generation began to view the Christmas hit in a way that reflected more George Orwell's 1984 than simple holiday fun. Gillespie's lyrics reinforced the idea that Big Brother is always watching. In a twenty-first-century context, it seems that Santa is so all-seeing that the jolly old elf must be affiliated with the Office of Homeland Security. After all, with no court orders, it seems, he has the right and ability to listen in on every conversation and observe every action of every child in the world. In that way, this song is almost frightening in its view of the holidays.

Yet, probably because Santa has such a benevolent image, it still works. Rather than scare us, "Santa Claus Is Coming to Town" invites us into a black-and-white world where being good is a goal with great rewards.

CAROL OF THE BELLS

hat's Christmas without all the bells? During the holidays, jingle bells and sleigh bells fill the air. Bells hang from car bumpers and are sewn onto hats. Street-corner Santas ring bells in the weeks before Christmas, and doorbells ring as friends and family drop by for holiday visits. On Christmas Eve and Christmas Day, the pealing of bells from steeples announces the arrival of the world's most beloved holiday. Bells are everywhere, so it seems only natural that one of the holiday's earliest hits is titled "Carol of the Bells."

It's hard to imagine Christmas without hearing the strains of this familiar song. Ironically, even though millions can hum the tune, most simply can't recall the title or name a recording artist who has cut it. It has become that rare song that no particular act can claim as its own, but that hasn't kept the hit from becoming one of the most recorded, requested, downloaded, and cherished carols of the season.

For two decades, "Carol of the Bells" was one of millions of obscure songs. Performed by choirs from time to time, mostly in Eastern Europe, the song didn't catch on in the United States. No one rushed out to incorporate the song into Hollywood movies or Broadway shows. It was a need for a new holiday tune for a radio orchestra that set in motion the events that led to "Carol of the Bells" becoming one of the most recorded instrumental songs and most performed choral anthems of the season. A hit that was almost thirty years in the making began in the office of a musician little known to Americans.

Mykola Dmytrovich Leontovych was thirty-nine years old and a national celebrity in the Ukraine when he sat down to compose the music for what has become one of the world's most popular Christmas carols. He called his work "Shchedryk," which means "The Generous One." Written as a choral standard to be sung *a cappella*, the song embraced the awakening of God's people to the beauty that can be found each day in his creation. The song's design is similar to that of Cat Stevens' chart-topping rock hit "Morning Has Broken." Leontovych's new work made its debut at Kiev University in December 1916, and the timing positioned the song as a Christmas standard, though the composer never meant for it to be a holiday anthem.

"Shchedryk" became popular in Ukraine because it was almost a "round." Choirs had fun with the song by having different people start at different times. Children loved it. The song was simple, but when performed by a choir, it could sound enticingly complicated.

Soon after "Shchedryk" gained popularity among choirs in the Ukraine, the royal family of Russia was overthrown,

Lenin rose to power, and the war to end all wars brought the globe into chaotic destruction. The Ukraine, which had been a unique nation with a distinct identity and culture, all but disappeared. Though the song was performed once by a visiting choir at Carnegie Hall in 1921, "Shchedryk" never caught on in the United States. As the influence of the U.S.S.R. took hold, the song lost popularity in the Ukraine. For Leontovych's ode to creation to find a rebirth, it would have to be rediscovered by a radio producer, remade into an instrumental piece, and coupled with a Christmas legend.

History is filled with fabrications that find their way into stories and songs. "Away in the Manger" was written two centuries ago by an American farmer, but around the world, millions believe it was penned by Martin Luther. Some Christmas programs show Luther singing this American song to his children! While "Carol of the Bells" has not spawned any false legends, a radio producer's coupling the song to the holiday season was the result of his parents telling him a legend about the night of Christ's birth, a tale likely created a thousand years after Jesus' arrival in a stable.

During the Middle Ages, bells were a vital communication network. Bells announced church services and served as a warning system for villagers. If an enemy was approaching, bells let the village know. Bells clamored as a signal that help was needed during a fire. Bells even announced births and deaths. For those who had little knowledge of history, it was natural to believe that bells had always been used in this fashion. This thinking led to the creation of a legend.

In the biblical description of the birth of Christ, attention is given to a bright star and heavenly host, but nowhere are bells being rung to announce the Messiah's birth. There is only one reference to bells in the Bible, and it's found in Zechariah's description of bells on horses. Somehow, by the Middle Ages, a legend that centered on the first Christmas and the tolling of bells was being accepted as truth.

This tale, which most Eastern European children could repeat, was that on the moment Christ was born, every bell in the world chimed. These bells rang together in a melodious manner that created a beautiful song, signifying that something special had just happened, and caused everyone on the planet to stop and marvel at what they'd heard.

Most believe that the legend of the ringing bells began at a fifth-century church in a children's service that included a play. As the play spread, the legend did too. Within five hundred years, many accepted it as the truth.

Around the time Leontovych composed "Shchedryk," Peter Wilhousky was part of the renowned Russian Cathedral Boys Choir in New York City. He eventually received a BA from what is now known as the Juilliard School of Music. His talent attracted music publishers and choirs. In his midthirties, he created the arrangement of "The Battle Hymn of the Republic" that paved the way for the Mormon Tabernacle Choir to become the world's best-known choral group. By 1936, Wilhousky was an arranger for the famed NBC radio network's symphony orchestra. While looking for new music to debut on NBC at Christmas, he discovered Leontovych's "Shchedryk."

When Wilhousky heard the simple harmonies of "Shchedryk" and noted the tune's bell-like cadence and sound, he thought of handbells. As he played the piano, he remembered a story his folks had told him — the legend of bells ringing out at Christ's birth. While keeping the essence of the original work, the American married the joy found in Leontovych's music with the Slavic legend. In 1936, with Wilhousky's new lyrics and arrangement embracing a Christmas theme, the song was reborn.

No longer a choral piece but now a melody arranged for an orchestra, the instrumental version made its American debut on NBC radio in the middle of the Depression. Within minutes of Wilhousky's orchestra playing the number, the switchboard lit up. Millions wanted to know where they could buy the music or the record. Within two years, the song became one of the most popular holiday sheet music compositions in the world. When Minna Louise Holman added new Christmas lyrics to Wilhousky's arrangement, the song became a holiday choral anthem.

Because it has been recorded by so many different artists, including the Carpenters, Celtic Woman, Andy Williams, Julie Andrews, and Mannheim Steamroller, no one can lay claim to having the definitive version of this century-old song. "Carol of the Bells" rings out each Christmas only because a legend and an inspired tune were married with an original beauty, grace, and majesty that few songs will ever know.

WHITE CHRISTMAS

*I*n America, it's rare for half of the country to see snow at Christmas. Even in the Midwestern plains of Iowa and Illinois, a white Christmas is not guaranteed. Yet for kids of all ages, December 25th and dreaming of snow go hand in hand. To capture this musically, it took a Russian immigrant and a singer from the state of Washington.

Irving Berlin has been called America's greatest songwriter. For eight decades, he composed hundreds of songs that ruled the charts, and he penned numbers that fueled popular Hollywood films and Broadway musicals. While other tunesmiths, such as Ira Gershwin, were more sophisticated, no one knew the American culture like Berlin. He had his finger on the pulse of the common man. He possessed an ability to shape music and lyrics that captured the hopes, dreams, and passions of millions.

The American composer was born into a family with little knowledge of the United States. Berlin was born Israel Baline and was five when the family immigrated to the United States to escape religious persecution in Russia. He grew up in the tenements of New York City and learned to sing from his father, a cantor in synagogues. At the age of thirteen, he watched illness claim his dad's life. To help raise money for his family, Berlin waited tables and performed songs in Tin Pan Alley eateries. At twenty-three, Berlin struck gold creating "Alexander's Ragtime Band," which initiated a worldwide dance craze and sold millions of copies of sheet music. Thanks to "Alexander," Berlin would never have to wait tables again.

While others may have relaxed and enjoyed their earnings, he constantly pushed himself to write new compositions. In his eighty-year career, he wrote more than fifteen hundred songs, including "Blue Skies," "God Bless America," and "There's No Business Like Show Business." His deep passion for music never waned, even as he approached his hundredth birthday.

The songwriter knew that Americans loved to celebrate holidays, from New Year's Day to Independence Day to Christmas. In the 1930s, a wealthy but restless Berlin developed a Broadway musical centered on holidays. Working with a basic plot outline, Berlin crafted songs to go with each special day. The number that most excited him was his Christmas song.

Berlin had been fascinated by Christmas since childhood. Though his family, being Jewish, did not celebrate what they saw as a Christian holiday, their neighbors did. Irving loved the music he heard and the gifts and lights he saw when he visited next door. He was equally drawn to Santa and the legends of the overgrown elf. What he loved most were the Christmas trees.

While Berlin's Christmas vision centered on the snowy New York holidays he remembered from his youth, he had spent enough time in Hollywood to realize that the holidays there were a great deal different. Those he knew in Los Angeles often sat around their swimming pools drinking martinis on December 25. Berlin was convinced these Westerners, who had no eggnog or snow, were missing the key elements that defined the holidays. This inspired him to compose an unusual and satirical ode to the Yuletide season for his play.

Berlin created a verse about the casual California view of the season. He worked in mixed drinks and lazy lounging by the pool. He also incorporated the idea that there had to be more to Christmas than just sunshine and kicking back. His California-based song slowly drifted into dreams of a holiday filled with the bite of the wind and a deep covering of snow. When set against the dark days of the Depression, this seemed the perfect jaded look at the season.

This version of "White Christmas" would never find an audience. Berlin's idea for a Broadway play about holidays didn't generate any excitement among backers, theater owners, or producers. He moved on to other projects. The idea would stay locked up for almost five years, until he dragged it out and reworked it into a screenplay.

As Berlin leafed through the songs he had penned several years before, he was pleased with almost everything but his Christmas song. Though America was not directly involved in fighting in 1941, most of the world was at war. Staying up all night, he removed the lines about booze and lazy days by the pool and replaced them with palm trees and sunny weather. The person singing his song would be enjoying the perfect Southern California day but feeling homesick for snow and a Christmas that reflected his youth.

Initially, he was excited about his new song, but the more he examined his holiday number, the more skeptical he became about the song's potential. He tried to develop another Christmas song to insert into the score but failed. With great trepidation, he took "White Christmas" to a meeting with his good friend and the film's star, Bing Crosby.

When Berlin tentatively sang through "White Christmas," Bing assured him the song was perfect. He didn't need to change a single word or note. Before the attack on Pearl Harbor, Crosby didn't consider debuting Berlin's new holiday song until the movie *Holiday Inn* was released in 1942. Yet as he experienced a holiday season filled with anxiety, he sensed he needed to sing "White Christmas" to bring a bit of comfort and hope to millions of Americans. He grabbed the sheet music and worked with his radio cast to bring the song to life on Christmas Day. The phone lines lit up as countless listeners begged Crosby to release a recording of "White Christmas." Since the holiday season was essentially over, the singer forgot the song until he went into the studio to cut it for the motion picture soundtrack the following May. Crosby took less than twenty minutes to record the single. Leaving the studio, he had no idea that those brief moments produced what would become the most popular recording in history.

Driven by both the movie *Holiday Inn* and family separations caused by the war, the single stayed at number 1 for a dozen weeks and won the Academy Award for best song of 1942.

Crosby later admitted that he didn't think the song would have a long shelf life. If it had been released at a different time, he might have been right. Yet in the early days of World War II, this secular carol resonated with millions of people like a prayer. Over the next twenty years, Bing Crosby's "White Christmas" landed on the charts fifteen more times. It even hit number 1 again in 1945 and 1946. Crosby's version of the Berlin song sold more than thirty million records and spawned a successful motion picture by the same name.

Bing Crosby died in 1977. Just before his death, he filmed a television special for the Christmas season. With his family around him, the man whose voice signified the beginning of the holidays sang "White Christmas" for the last time. There could not have been a better way for the singer to say farewell.

I'll Be Home for Christmas

*O*ne mistake made by many speakers and writers is thinking a message must be lengthy to be dynamic. Far from it. Abraham Lincoln's best-known speech was just a few minutes long, while some of the great works of Mark Twain are short stories. In contemporary music, brief and to the point is almost always better. One holiday song, "I'll Be Home for Christmas," celebrates the brevity of a great message and inspiring music.

While the message in "I'll Be Home for Christmas" is simple, the song's history is muddled in a complex controversy. Almost seven decades after the tune became a treasured part of the holidays, there is still an unsolved mystery about who came up with the idea for this Christmas classic and who is most responsible for crafting the memorable words.

James Kimble "Kim" Gannon was a New Yorker. Born in Brooklyn in 1900, this bright young man graduated from the Albany Law School and earned his license in 1934. Even as Gannon worked his way through dusty law books, an old hobby continued to pull him in another direction.

Gannon loved to play with words. His poetry reflected the urban world he saw. In time, he refined his work enough to become known in New York's music publishing world and began to pitch his songs. In 1939, Gannon's "For Tonight" was published. Recorded by Charlie Bennett, the song made it to number 15 on the hit parade. Though it was not a huge hit, "For Tonight" convinced the attorney to give up legal work and cast his lot in the highly competitive world of entertainment. This proved to be a good move when Dick Todd took Gannon's "Angel in Disguise" into the top 20 a year later. Though he would never be mistaken for Irving Berlin, Gannon produced several songs for minor movies, hit the charts a half-dozen times, and established a career as a pretty solid tunesmith.

One of Gannon's friends was Walter Kent, a man searching for a collaborator. He understood music and knew his way around a keyboard. Though Kent never created a long list of hits, in 1941, on the eve of World War II, he and Nat Burton penned a monster. "The White Cliffs of Dover" became one of the best-selling songs of the decade and made Kent a respected man around town.

In 1942, at an out-of-the-way New York diner on an evening just before Christmas, Kent met with Gannon and another songwriter named Buck Ram. As they ate and swapped stories of their latest musical efforts, the thirty-five-year-old Ram told Gannon and Kent about a song he had written for his mother almost two decades before. The lyrics were a testament to how much he missed her while he was away at college. Ram had the holiday song with him and showed it to the men as they spoke.

Legend has it that Gannon looked it over while Kent noted the irony that a teenage Ram would pen a Christmas song for his Jewish mother. As Kent was also a Jew, the comment was meant not as a racial or religious slight but as simply a humorous observation. Supposedly, Ram laughed, pointed out that another Jew had written "White Christmas," and assured the two friends that his holiday song was a hit in the making. In a year, he predicted, they would see "I'll Be Home for Christmas (Though Just a Memory)" find a place on the hit parade. The conversation shifted and the meal continued.

That night, Ram did not arrive home with his copy of his song. He assumed he had left it on the table at the diner. Because his publisher had a copyrighted copy, he put the missing sheet music out of his mind and went about the business of trying to create a hit that would pay the bills until his Christmas song was recorded and released. Testimony from a later civil trial confirmed that Kent and Gannon did not see Ram again until a courtroom appearance almost ten months later.

The following summer, Kent and Gannon got together to brainstorm. Of the ideas that they jotted down on paper, "I'll Be Home for Christmas (If Only in My Dreams)" seemed to have the most potential. Though it had essentially the same title as Ram's song, at the time, the songwriting team thought their new composition was based on a much different theme and therefore had no resemblance to the one they had seen at the diner. They copyrighted the number in late August and, after Kent reworked his melody and arrangement and Gannon polished his words, they copyrighted a second version of the song in late September. With his background in law, Gannon should have realized that employing the same basic title for his lyrics as had Buck Ram spelled trouble. He later claimed he hadn't even thought of Ram's song when he got the idea for his song. His inspiration came from a war that had separated families.

Kent and Gannon's publisher sent a demo record of "I'll Be Home for Christmas" to Bing Crosby. The crooner loved it and rushed into the studio with the John Scott Trotter Orchestra to cut the Kent/Gannon original. When Ram found out that Crosby had recorded a song with the same title as the one he had written, he could not believe the coincidence. Nothing would have come of it, since lots of songs had the same titles, if Ram had not seen Kent's and Gannon's names listed as the composers of the new "I'll Be Home for Christmas." Though he had not heard the record, Ram was sure the songwriting duo had stolen his idea from the sheet music he had left at the diner almost a year before. He retained a lawyer and filed suit. Within weeks, he was in court demanding he be given credit as the writer of the new holiday number.

In court, it was discovered that the two songs had little in common other than the main title. Because of the dinner date and the discussion of Ram's earlier song over the meal, and because of the missing piece of sheet music, the court ruled that Ram's name be added to the copyright and that the royalties be split three ways. The ruling did not happen in time for Ram's name to appear on the initial release of Crosby's single, however, and the first pressing went out with just Gannon and Kent listed as writers.

"I'll Be Home for Christmas" hit number 3 on the charts in 1943. The song returned to the playlists several times over the next few decades and was recorded by a host of other artists. Though Gannon and Kent never admitted that Ram should have had any part of their work, there can be little doubt that without his providing at least a seed of inspiration, the song never would have been written.

A decade later, the frustrated Ram found his niche as a songwriter and earned much more acclaim than had the duo he shared credit with on the Christmas classic. In the early days of rock and roll, he penned hit after hit, including, "Only You," "The Great Pretender," and "Twilight Time."

No matter where the idea for the song came from, Gannon and Kent deserve credit for tapping into the mood of a nation when they wrote "I'll Be Home for Christmas." One of the most interesting lines in Gannon's short but poetic lyrics often confuses listeners today. Written from the viewpoint of the singer — a lonely person who might not make it back this holiday season — is a simple request to have "presents on the tree." When he penned his words, Gannon was forty-three. The Christmases of his youth were much simpler than those of our modern age. Presents were fewer and much smaller. In fact, most were so small that they were not placed under the tree but tied to the branches. While the meaning and emotion of "I'll Be Home for Christmas" has not changed in the seven decades since it was written, some of the traditions have. In that way, the song is a wonderful glimpse of the holiday as it used to be.

Born in the summer in New York City, and tied up in a court case that almost canceled its initial release, "I'll Be Home for Christmas" is one of the simplest Christmas carols ever written. There is an introduction, a single verse, and a chorus, yet those few simple lines became a prayer for a nation uncertain about the outcome of World War II. The song still works today because home is where Christmas comes to life and home is where the holiday takes us, even if it's only in our dreams.

Have Yourself
a Merry Little Christmas

*J*udy Garland owned her songs. Garland may not have had the publishing rights, but when she performed a song, she became her music and her music became her. Few tried to cover her hits. Those who did discovered they could not compete. Once she placed her stamp on a song, the mark could not be removed.

Many are surprised that Judy didn't have a parade of holiday hits. She could have become the female Bing Crosby when it came to Christmas songs. Her unique style and haunting voice, coupled with the fact that she introduced beloved standards such as "Over the Rainbow" and "The Trolley Song," lead many to believe that Garland was a huge recording sensation. Nothing could be further from the truth. Dinah Shore and Jo Stafford, recording in the same period as Garland, both landed in the top 40 seventy-five times. Shore had four number 1 hits, while Stafford scored more than a dozen. However, Garland hit the charts just seventeen times and never scored a number 1 record.

Judy did not consider herself a recording artist. Neither did her label. Decca Records saw Garland as a movie star who sang, not a singer who acted. The songs she released often came from her films. Many of Judy's movies are classics and replayed in television outlets. Each new generation is exposed to Judy's music, and thus these films keep the interest in her recordings alive, while Shore and Stafford have largely been forgotten.

Today, "Over the Rainbow" is viewed as an iconic musical treasure, but when it was released, the song climbed to only number 5 on the charts. "Have Yourself a Merry Little Christmas" was recorded only because it was a part of the score of an MGM musical. Judy's success with one of the most beloved and best-selling Christmas singles of all time cuts against the grain of her track record as a vocalist.

Garland, who was not a songwriter, had a huge impact on the lyrics of this holiday hit. Her input and stubborn resolve may have saved this song from obscurity.

The 1940s were a golden age for songwriters in Hollywood. Studios were trying to keep up with the public's demand for musicals. During World War II, any actor or actress who could sing and dance had value. Those who could pen music for these stars were also coveted. It was a great time to be a tunesmith.

Hugh Martin and Ralph Blane formed a winning composition team whose hits set them apart from their peers. In Hollywood terms, they were top-shelf. Their success and earnings proved it. Because of their track record, stacks of scripts weighed down their desks, sent by producers and directors begging them to create the songs for upcoming projects. Over the course of their careers, they penned musical scores for films including *Girl Crazy, Broadway Rhythm,* and *Gentlemen Prefer Blondes.* They also teamed up to create music for Broadway and radio. Many of their tunes were cut by artists such as Frank Sinatra, Dinah Shore, Lena Horne, Ethel Merman, Mickey Rooney, and Ann Miller. In 1943, MGM paid the duo handsomely to score their musical *Meet Me in St. Louis.*

What Martin and Blane couldn't have guessed was that one of their songs would be rejected by the film's star. In fact, the twenty-two-year-old film veteran threatened to walk off the set if the lyrics were not changed.

Filmed in the midst of World War II, *Meet Me in St. Louis* starred Mary Astor, Leon Ames, June Lockhart, and Margaret O'Brien. Still, everyone knew that it was Judy Garland's film. Judy wanted *Meet Me in St. Louis* to be the film that took her career over the rainbow. She was the headlining star and needed the role to bridge the gap between juvenile sensation and respected adult actress.

At a point in the storyline when Judy's character, Esther, learns her family is moving from Missouri to New York, she realizes she might never again see the young man she loves. She attempts to soothe the nerves of a little sister who believes that Santa will not be able to find them when they move. Even as she comforts her sister, the older girl's heart breaks. Although it's a beautiful Christmas Eve night, both sisters consider December 24 the end of the world. Martin and Blane wrote what they believed was one of their best songs for this pivotal moment of the film. The songwriters even gave this ode to lost love a holiday touch.

The song Martin and Blane wrote contained a line that Judy found horrifying. When she read, "Have yourself a merry Christmas / it may be your last / next year we will be living in the past," she threw down the sheet music in disgust.

Martin and Blane had captured the feeling of two young lovers about to be torn apart. The film was set in a time before mass transportation. The distance between St. Louis and New York likely meant the lovers would never see each other again. As a part of the film's script, the line worked perfectly.

But Judy was not thinking about the script — she was thinking about the times. This was World War II. Millions were separated from loved ones, and some would never be reunited. The line would hit them much differently than it would if America were at peace. Judy refused to give families praying for a future holiday reunion a message that indicated that their best Christmases might be behind them. Backed by Vincente Minnelli, who was the film's director and her future husband, Garland sent the song back for a rewrite.

Though neither believed it was in the best interest of their composition, Martin and Blane wrote a new, far more upbeat opening. The verse was framed by the happy line "Let your heart be light / from now on our troubles will be out of sight." Judy embraced the revised "Have Yourself a Merry Little Christmas" as a prayer for the millions wanting nothing more than to be together again with their loved ones for Christmas. It was as if she were saying, "Don't worry, the war will be over soon, and all of these bad moments will be forever behind us." She knew this was a message America wanted and needed to hear.

Film fans both smiled and cried when they saw Judy's performance of "Have Yourself a Merry Little Christmas" on the silver screen. Decca released the song's single, which was just as powerful. On the night Judy first sang the song to troops at the Hollywood Canteen, many battle-tested soldiers cried. When weary soldiers in Europe and the Pacific heard the song over their unit's radio, they clung to its lyrics as if the words defined their dreams. It was as if Judy were singing directly to them, bringing hope wrapped in a package that was both significant and beautiful.

How did Garland know that Martin and Blane's song needed a new slant? What gave her the insight? Personal experience. Working for the USO, an entertainment organization that brought big-name acts to the war theater to entertain the troops, she had performed for thousands of men in uniform. At each of those shows, the men screamed out requests for "Over the Rainbow." To them, "over the rainbow" was not about Oz; it was about home. If they could just get to the other side of the rainbow, then everything they knew and loved would be back in their lives. That was the message Judy wanted these men to hear in her Christmas song. It might have taken a rewrite, but Martin and Blane delivered a present that has now touched generations of people with hope during the holiday season and beyond.

9
THE CHRISTMAS SONG

*U*ntil the mid-1940s, not only was Christmas always pictured in song, film, and seasonal cards with snow, but those singing holiday classics on radio and in motion pictures were just as white as that snow. During this period, integration rarely hit mainstream radio outlets and was not incorporated into popular Christmas music. A songwriting team and a former jazz pianist would change all that in the days just after World War II. When the nation was looking forward to knowing peace and security, the Christmas color line was crossed.

Mel Tormé was a Chicago-born, Jewish jazz singer who grew up in show business. He first sang on the radio at the age of four, landed acting roles on national radio series when in grade school, and penned a hit song for the Harry James Orchestra in his teens. After graduating from high school, he toured with different bands, appeared in a Frank Sinatra movie, and with Les Baxter and Henry Mancini formed a trio known as the Meltones. This singing group became one of the first jazz-influenced vocal bands.

Over the next five decades, Tormé composed a long list of hits for other acts, sold millions of records on his own, played supporting roles in dozens of movies and television shows, penned best-selling books, and, when he grew bored with show business, flew airplanes as a commercial pilot. Tormé is best remembered as playing himself on the TV show *Night Court*. His parody of a lounge singer was so funny that millions never realized the real talents of the man called "The Velvet Fog." Without his holiday song, a portion of his success would never have transpired.

In 1946, Tormé was assigned to compose two musical movie scores with his close friend, lyricist Robert Wells. As the sun beat down and temperatures hit triple digits, neither man felt like writing. Sitting in front of fans and drinking pitchers of iced lemonade, they killed time talking about winter days in New England. Wells even scribbled down a few thoughts of colder times. He set his notebook on the piano as he got up to walk outside. A few moments later, Tormé picked up the notebook and was immediately inspired.

"I saw a spiral pad on his piano with four lines written in pencil," Tormé wrote in his autobiography *It Wasn't All Velvet*. "They started, 'Chestnuts roasting ... Jack Frost nipping ... Yuletide carols ... Folks dressed up like Eskimos.' Bob didn't think he was writing a song lyric. He said he thought if he could immerse himself in winter, he could cool off."

While Evans saw nothing in the lines he had written but an attempt to keep cool, Mel caught a glimpse of a song. With Tormé leading the charge, they forgot about the work

61

they had been hired to do and composed a new song in just forty minutes. Tormé felt that Nat King Cole was the man who best fit "The Christmas Song."

Tormé had fallen in love with jazz as a child and had worked with African Americans all his life. To him, skin was little more than a fashion accessory. He had no problem with a black man cutting his and Wells' newest composition. If he had considered the reality of how hard it was to get radio stations to play music performed by men and women of color, he might have jumped into the car and driven to Bing Crosby's house. Instead, Tormé grabbed Wells and rushed to his car to find Nat King Cole.

Tormé had visited Cole's house many times, and the singer was not surprised to see him arrive at his door unannounced. Tormé played and sang the new holiday number. Impressed by this new, jazzy, cool take on Christmas, Cole asked the songwriters to put a hold on the piece until he could get into the studio to cut it. Tormé and Wells agreed, leaving the music and lyrics with Cole.

Cole was almost thirty and had had enough success as a jazz pianist and vocalist to live comfortably in Los Angeles, but he was not a household name. While his smooth baritone was mesmerizing, the color of his skin limited the way Capitol Records could market him. Many stations, especially in the Midwest and South, refused to play his music once they discovered Cole was black.

In the integrated clubs where he performed, his great sense of style and dynamic stage presence earned him the nickname King. Seizing on this title and tying it to the old English nursery rhyme "Old King Cole," Capitol marketed the singer as Nat "King" Cole. Under that title, he had scored a few minor hits, including "Straighten Up and Fly Right" and "Get Your Kicks on Route 66." The record company executives felt that if he had been white, Cole would have topped the charts with those two releases.

Within days of Tormé bringing "The Christmas Song" to his home, Cole rearranged the song and cut it for Capitol Records. Cole was genuinely fearful that if Bing Crosby or Dinah Shore heard the song first, they would beat him to the punch. With the tracks laid down, the question that haunted the label and the singer was, would Americans buy a Christmas song from a black artist?

A few weeks before "The Christmas Song" released, Capitol shipped a new Cole recording, "(I Love You) For Sentimental Reasons," to radio stations and record outlets. This ballad smashed the radio color line in the same way that Jackie Robinson broke the color line in baseball a few months later. Cole moved to the top of the *Billboard* charts for six weeks and earned the hottest-selling record of the immediate postwar era. Fans longed for another classic from the King. The timing for the release of his new holiday recording couldn't have been better.

Thanks to Nat King Cole, Christmas had color! The song marked the first time thousands of white Americans plopped down the money to purchase a black man's holiday record. The success generated by "The Christmas Song" opened the door for Lou Rawls, Ray Charles, Eartha Kitt, and Ethel Waters to put their own spins on holiday classics.

No matter how well Bing Crosby, Judy Garland, or even Mel Tormé preformed "The Christmas Song," it was considered a Nat King Cole classic. Every other recording was just a pale imitation.

When people around the world listen to Nat King Cole sing about what makes Christmas so special, they hear his rich baritone voice describing cold noses, hot chestnuts, and Yuletide carols. One of the most famous modern Christmas recordings brought together a Jewish American and an African American to create Christmas imagery that has rarely been equaled and never surpassed. To many, "The Christmas Song" is one of the greatest moments in musical history because it helped paint Christmas in its true colors.

10

HERE COMES SANTA CLAUS (RIGHT DOWN SANTA CLAUS LANE)

*M*any of today's most popular Christmas classics were introduced during World War II and in the years following. Music, more noticeably than literature and film, seemed to bring the nation real hope during the insecure days of war. Music was a uniting force. The songs that were introduced during this time seemed to push deep into listeners' hearts and linger longer than songs released during times of peace. Holiday music created a very emotional and lasting connection between those fighting in faraway lands and their loved ones at home. During this period, music — much more than gifts or decorations — defined the holiday season. One of those touched deeply by the songs of Christmas during his time in the service was the singer/actor who would pen the first postwar Christmas hit.

A Texas-born telegraph operator, Gene Autry picked up a guitar and changed his fortunes in the early days of the Great

Depression. His big break came when a stranger walked into the train station in the town of Sapulpa, Oklahoma, and heard the young, transplanted Okie singing a Jimmie Rogers number. As soon as Autry finished his hillbilly ode, the stranger said, "You're pretty good. I'm proud to meet you. My name is Will Rogers." Over the next hour, the two became friends as they sang a long list of popular songs. Just before Will left the station on an eastbound train, the Oklahoma humorist told the telegraph operator, "You need to be on radio. You have too much talent to spend your life out here."

Will Rogers had already touched America on the stages of Broadway in New York. Gene Autry headed in the same direction. The singer found that the early 1930s New York landscape offered few opportunities and little hope for entertainers — especially those with a country twang. After failing in the Big Apple, Autry wandered into the Windy City, where his unique country sound fit in with a community known for its stockyards. By 1934, the former telegraph operator had scored a few hit records for the Melotone label and negotiated a spot on a Chicago radio station.

WLS was the home of America's hottest live music program — *National Barn Dance*. Millions throughout more than thirty states and much of Canada tuned in each week. It was a radio destination point, and the acts appearing on *Barn Dance* had immense followings. The bright audio spotlight afforded by WLS was the break the Oklahoma cowboy needed. With his charm, polite manners, and smooth western voice, he won over hundreds of thousands of fans, sold boxes of records for his label, and caught the ear of talent scouts from Los Angeles. When Hollywood discovered that Autry was a good-looking man who could ride a horse and sing, Mascot Pictures offered him a contract. Within five years of the day when Will Rogers encouraged him to pursue a dream, Autry was on his way to becoming a major star.

In 1934, Autry landed his first major part in a B movie, playing a singer named Gene. His clean-cut, all-American style was perfect for a time when the Soviet Union and Nazi Germany threatened the ideals of the Western world and church leaders demanded that Hollywood offer pictures that embraced moral themes. Though not the first singing cowboy, he became the most popular, cranking out scores of pictures, each with pretty much the same plot. In these flicks aimed at young people, Autry played himself, uncovered a plot by the bad guys, rounded them up and put them in jail, rescued a pretty starlet, sang a few songs, and rode off into the sunset on his horse, Champion.

While other actors hated being tossed into a niche where their fans were children, Autry relished it. He had no desire to be the next Clark Gable and enjoyed his status as the adult role model for millions of grade-school kids. During the 1930s, his patriotism and straightforward values were spot-on for the parts he played. Millions of kids who went to his movies every Saturday and listened to his radio program saw Gene as a big brother or second father.

By marketing himself to children, during a time when many people were drowning in poverty, Autry became a millionaire. He was at the height of his success when the Japanese attacked Pearl Harbor. Without considering the cost to his career, Autry immediately enlisted in the Army Air Corps. He served as a commander in Burma and became as true a hero during World War II as he had been on the silver screen.

When the war ended, Autry faced a question that troubled scores of others in the world of entertainment. Would the public remember him? After all, it had been almost four years since his fans had seen or heard him, and most of those fans had now grown up from kids into teenagers. Worst of all, a new generation of grade-schoolers likely didn't have any idea who he was.

In 1946, because of his prewar success, Autry was one of the special guests in the Hollywood Christmas Parade. This would be the appearance that would allow Autry to gauge his star power. Riding his horse, Champion, Autry was overwhelmed by the response of the thousands who lined the parade route. As far as he could see, children were jumping up and down, pointing their fingers, screaming, and saluting. He was thrilled! It seemed they had not forgotten their hero. As he rode past one vocal young boy, Autry trotted closer to the curb and said, "Howdy." Strangely, the kid didn't respond. In fact, he looked right past the finely dressed movie star and pointed to something behind Autry. Turning his head, the cowboy noted who was behind him in the parade: a big man with a white beard, dressed in a red suit. Smiling, Gene leaned closer to the child in an attempt to hear what he was saying.

"Mom, look, here comes Santa Claus!"

Gene Autry had been upstaged. The kids had not been screaming for him; they'd been yelling for St. Nick!

After the parade, the movie star went home and called his friend, composer Oakley Halderman. Autry told Halderman the story of the parade where Santa had stolen the cowboy's spotlight. In the midst of his story, the cowboy star laughed. "Yep, they kept saying, 'Here comes Santa Claus.'"

"Gene," Halderman replied, "this sounds like a song to me."

Within days, the two men had penned what would become the holiday classic and Autry's first top 10 record in a decade. More than just becoming one of the best-loved songs of Christmas, "Here Comes Santa Claus" would also reestablish Autry as a huge Hollywood star and spin his career in a new direction.

After its release in the late fall of 1947, stores could not keep the song in stock. "Here Comes Santa Claus" climbed into the top 10 of the pop playlists and hit the top 5 on the country charts. The record became the best-selling children's single of the year and even reentered the *Billboard* listings every holiday season for the next decade. Many predicted that "Here Comes Santa Claus" would surpass the popularity of "Back in the Saddle" and "That Silver-Haired Daddy of Mine" and become Autry's signature song.

More than six decades later, "Here Comes Santa Claus" remains one of the most requested Christmas standards and has been recorded by hundreds of artists, from Doris Day to Willie Nelson to Bob Dylan. Why has it come to mean so much to so many all around the planet? Perhaps because this classic holiday offering is simple, direct, and honest, much like the man who introduced the secular carol. United by their generosity and their love for the world's children, the legendary Santa and the real Gene Autry were very much alike, so it's no surprise that an American cowboy became a vital part of holidays all over the globe.

11

LET IT SNOW

*O*ver the course of just a few months in 1945 and 1946, one love ballad, now deeply associated with Christmas, became a major hit by several different artists. The chart topper, written by two legendary song scribes on an ironically hot summer day, remains one of the most recorded and beloved songs of the Christmas season even though it makes no mention of the holiday. "Let It Snow" is a simple reminder of the promise of love waiting under every sprig of mistletoe.

In the summer of 1945, Sammy Cahn and Jule Styne were in a Hollywood meeting with their publisher. Over cool drinks, intended to fend off a stifling heat wave, the men worked out the details of a contract. The easygoing Cahn suggested the group should adjourn to the beach and catch some rays. He argued that it was far too hot to work. According to James Adam Richliano, in his book *Angels We Have Heard*, Styne waved him off with the comment, "If you want to stay cool, we can write a song about winter." The battle of wills that followed helped create the first major adult holiday hit of the post–World War II era.

Styne was a workaholic driven to create. He was born in London, England, in 1905, the son of Jewish immigrants who had moved to Britain from the Ukraine seeking freedom and opportunity. With little promise in England, they repacked and headed across the Atlantic to Chicago. Styne showed an aptitude for piano. Working hours each day, he honed his skills and became popular at neighborhood gatherings. Word of his talent spread. By his teens, he was playing with the Chicago Symphony.

Styne began to compose at the Chicago Musical College and, after graduating, formed a dance band. He worked his way across America one gig at a time until he landed in Hollywood. There, supposedly through an introduction by Frank Sinatra, he met Sammy Cahn. Forming a team, the men began to pen songs for the movies.

Cahn shared Styne's Jewish roots. Born Samuel Cohen in New York City in 1913, Cahn showed a flair for poetry and music at an early age. Hoping to provide a career path for their boy to escape the poverty that had ensnared them, his immigrant parents enrolled the boy in music lessons. He mastered piano and violin and began to compose original songs. As a teen, he pitched his music to Broadway publishers and changed his name to Cahn to avoid being confused with a comedian of the era. He quickly found a degree of success and moved west to write for motion pictures.

Unlike Styne, Cahn was a carefree soul. His first wife was a showgirl. He enjoyed hanging out with friends and sharing laughs. The two men, similar and yet different, kept each other in check. Over the course of their career, this partnership produced four Academy Awards and a string of hits. If Cahn had won the tug-of-war to go to the beach that summer day in 1945, the holiday season would have been far less romantic.

In a stifling hot room, Styne sat down at a piano and began to work out a melody line that he thought sounded "cool." Cahn, who realized that his dreams of sand and surf were going to have to wait, turned his thoughts to winter. Looking out the window at the California sun baking the landscape, he whispered, "Let it snow." As both men had grown up in parts of the world where snow often paralyzed travel, they began to exchange memories of being snowed in. A romantic at heart, Cahn transformed these thoughts into a mini-movie script about a man and woman trapped by a blizzard but warmed by a fire. The story's hook was that the pair was too much in love to say goodbye.

"Let It Snow" was short and sweet, with only sixteen lines. Perhaps it was not further developed because Cahn was so anxious to get to the beach. The major plot points were a blizzard, a warm fire, popcorn, and two lovers who thought they were blessed by having the snow strand them together. In retrospect, as catchy as it was, if "Let It Snow" had been penned by two struggling amateurs, it might not have been noticed. But folks lined up to cut anything that Cahn and Styne wrote, so even the simple "Let It Snow" had no problem finding an artist willing to take a chance on it.

Forty-four-year-old Vaughn Monroe was the leader of

one of the nation's hottest bands. A Pennsylvania native, he had formed his group on the East Coast in the 1930s and quickly established a following in the Boston area. The hardworking Monroe traveled from coast to coast, wowing crowds more with his voice than with his trumpet. By 1940, he had landed a record deal with RCA. Beginning with "There I Go," he reeled off five number 1 songs and charted twenty-five times in the next four years.

In 1945, Monroe was looking for new material. He sensed that upbeat love ballads were going to play well in a country embracing peace for the first time in four years. To him, a man who had grown up shoveling deep Pennsylvania snow, Cahn and Styne's winter number was a natural that fit his style as well as the national mood. Monroe jumped at the chance to be the first to record "Let It Snow."

Monroe cut "Let It Snow" with his band on Halloween day. Though it was ready for release within a week, RCA held the record until just after Thanksgiving. The timing couldn't have been better. GIs had come back by the millions from overseas, the world was at peace, and romance was in the air. "Let It Snow" became the love ballad that touched the country's heart during that first postwar Christmas season.

Monroe's record topped the charts just after Christmas and held the lofty position for five weeks. In February, the song's popularity began to wane. But just because Monroe's cut was dropping off the charts didn't mean other versions of "Let It Snow" weren't being played. The song made the top 20 three more times in the winter of 1946.

The second-most played version during that initial year of release was by Connee Boswell. Boswell began singing with her sisters in Missouri while in her teens. She landed a record contract in the early 1930s and scored a number 1 hit with "Bob White." Other hits followed. Boswell had a smooth alto voice, a warm smile, and dynamic wit. What made her unique was that a childhood illness had left her in a wheelchair. At a time when few handicapped people gained entrance into the mainstream world, she lived her dreams. A favorite duet partner of Bing Crosby and a huge star on radio, Boswell perhaps made her most important mark as an example rather than a singer. Her fortitude and positive attitude became an important symbol during the waning days of World War II as many Americans came home with crippling injuries. Having achieved success despite her handicap, she provided inspiration in ways few others could, and Boswell relished that role. Thus, her version of "Let It Snow" spoke to listeners in two distinct ways. The initial impact came because it was a great cut. The second, more lasting impact was created because it showed that Americans could overcome anything with enough determination and grit. Her story demonstrated that even those who had come back from the war scarred and badly injured still had potential.

By the 1950s, "Let It Snow" was firmly established as a holiday favorite. Because it had been a hit for various acts in its initial year of release, no single artist could claim the song as his or her own. In the 1960s, Dean Martin changed that. The crooner cut a version of "Let It Snow" that quickly became his signature holiday song. Infused with fresh energy from a Christmas album release and the publicity of a performance on Martin's popular television show, "Let It Snow" again became a hit. Thanks to that exposure, the song is now usually thought of as Dean's Christmas song.

By 2010, "Let It Snow" had been established as one of the ten most popular holiday songs. Its association with Christmas is now so well defined that just hearing it conjures up images of trees, cards, presents, and Santa. Few listeners realize that "Let It Snow" is a simple love ballad about a blizzard, a couple, and shared popcorn, with no mention of the trappings of Christmas. Sammy Cahn and Jule Styne, writing it on a hot summer day, could never have anticipated that it would become one of the holiday's most beloved hits.

12

SLEIGH RIDE

One of the most recorded hits of the holiday season owes its popularity to America's most beloved symphony orchestra. Without the Boston Pops, there would likely not have been a "Sleigh Ride," and without Arthur Fiedler, few might know the Boston Pops.

Until 1930, the Boston Pops Orchestra used various conductors during their performances, and the Pops' musical direction changed often. As the Depression strangled global financial markets, major orchestras across the nation took big hits. Donations from the wealthy dried up, and many couldn't make ends meet and folded.

Those governing the Boston Pops realized that to withstand the economic downturn, they needed a creative mind and charismatic leader at the helm. They hired a thirty-five-year-old Boston native to transform the staid, traditional orchestra. Rather than stay for a year or less like past conductors, Arthur Fiedler remained with the group five decades. Under his baton, the Boston Pops changed the personality and direction of orchestra music. From a local group of musicians playing for Boston's upper class, they were transformed into the favorite orchestra of the nation.

Although a highly trained, world-traveled, and much-respected conductor and musician, Fiedler sensed that for the Pops to survive, he needed to target a new audience. Until 1930, the Pops had reached out to the social elite. Their concerts were society affairs that brought out wealthy citizens parading in their finest dress. These programs were always held in the grandest concert halls, and ticket prices were too steep for the common factory worker. The music was as highbrow as the clientele. The poorer classes viewed these concerts as stuffy and, for most, boring.

During the Depression, the idle rich had become an almost endangered species. The numbers of people attending concerts plummeted. Sensing a need to develop a new group of patrons for orchestra music, Fiedler turned tradition upside down by taking modern jazz and popular music and rearranging it for the Pops. He staged free concerts for the masses. He not only changed the demographic for orchestra music; he likely saved the Boston Pops.

One area that Fiedler used to expand the fan base and pay the bills was recorded music. The conductor began recording songs, such as George Gershwin's "Rhapsody in Blue," and releasing them as singles. Radio stations across America put the Pops' versions of modern tunes into heavy rotation, and by the late 1930s the group was the most popular orchestra in the world. The Pops were known as the classical band of regular people, and everyone seemed to love them.

As the popularity of the orchestra grew, Fiedler felt a need to spotlight original music, and the man he turned to was Leroy Anderson. Born in Cambridge, Anderson learned piano from his mother, studied music in elementary school, and attended Harvard. He received his master's from that university just as Fiedler took over the Pops. Anderson could speak Swedish, Danish, Norwegian, Icelandic, German, French, Italian, and Portuguese. Because of these skills, he was recruited for careers in the diplomatic service, but instead he opted to stay in Boston, where he directed the Harvard Band, served as a minister of music at a church, and created arrangements for local music groups. In the midthirties, Fiedler met the busy musician, and Anderson began to work with the Pops toward the end of the decade.

Just as his career as a composer was beginning to take off, Anderson entered the military during World War II. While serving overseas, he continued to compose. In 1945, he wrote a piece he called "The Syncopated Clock," which became one of the most beloved and well-known instrumental pieces of the era. Anderson's "Blue Tango" also reflected this blend of classical and popular music and sold a million records. Returning to civilian life, Anderson found himself one of the country's most sought-after composers of instrumental music.

In 1946, during one of New England's warmest days of the year, Anderson tried to recreate a winter's sleigh ride in music. He developed a melody that fit a cold day, and added other elements to simulate the feel of traveling in a horse-drawn sleigh. His whole object was for every listener to see the picture of winter as they heard the music.

When writing, Anderson did not pause to even consider lyrics. In his mind, his songs didn't need them. "Blue Tango," "The Syncopated Clock," and "Sleigh Ride" painted the needed picture without words. He felt the story they told through music was that obvious.

Anderson did not rush a song. While he wrote "Sleigh Ride" in 1946, he didn't finish polishing the tune until two years later. Only when he felt he had covered all the angles and possessed a canvas of notes so clear that anyone could sense its meaning did he cut a piano demo record. He likely gave it to Fiedler. Later he supplied the full arrangement to the conductor.

Fiedler loved the song. He immediately sensed its potential. Once he was confident of the final arrangement, the conductor scheduled a recording session for the Boston Pops. Though not considered a true holiday number, it was released during the early winter and became associated with Christmas. The record peaked on the charts on Christmas Eve.

A Lithuanian Jewish immigrant put the finishing touches on Anderson's musical sleigh ride. Michael Pashelinsky was nearing his fiftieth birthday when he heard Anderson's new song. Raised in New York and known to the music world as Mitchell Parish, he had emerged as a topflight lyricist in the 1920s. During his first two decades as a writer, the song scribe penned such classics and chart toppers as "Star Dust," "Stars Fell on Alabama," and "Moonlight Serenade." Though he could write with others and had little problem composing lyrics before even hearing a musical line, Parish was most comfortable creating words for previously written melodies.

Parish didn't have to work too hard on the song's theme. The music's imagery was so strong that the verses almost wrote themselves. It took the writer a while to edit the final lyrics into verses with the alliteration needed to match the genius he saw in the music. The Boston Pops' version was still ringing in the ears of millions when the lyricist shipped his new version to his publisher. A host of artists wanted to cut a lyrical version of "Sleigh Ride," but the legendary Andrews Sisters got there first. Bing Crosby followed with his take on the song about a winter adventure in the snow. Thanks to these and a dozen other versions fighting for radio play, millions were soon humming Anderson's melody and singing Parish's words.

According to the American Society of Composers, Authors and Publishers (ASCAP), "Sleigh Ride" has been performed and recorded by a wider array of musical artists than any other piece in the history of Western music. Considering it charted on popular radio playlists only once, this is an amazing feat!

Today, the most played vocal version with Mitchell Parish's lyrics was recorded by Andy Williams. Still, the version embraced by millions each holiday season is the original by the Boston Pops. Played as intended by its composer, this version paints the truest picture and captures the widest range of emotions associated with a crisp winter's ride through the New England snow. Arthur Fiedler always believed it was the perfect blend of classical and popular music, but it is also much more. No instrumental holiday song is closer to a rich piece of finished art than this masterpiece painted on a musical canvas.

13

RUDOLPH
THE RED-NOSED REINDEER

udolph the Red-Nosed Reindeer might be the only children's book ever transformed into a classic holiday song. In fact, the song eclipsed the book in popularity, and today, according to the statistics, this beloved holiday jingle claims the runner-up spot as the top-selling Christmas single of all time.

In 1938, as the Great Depression wound down and the prospect of better times loomed on the horizon, Bob May was looking toward another bleak Christmas. An advertising copywriter for Montgomery Ward in Chicago, Illinois, May was on the brink of exhaustion. After fighting cancer for two years, his wife, Evelyn, was now losing the battle. She was in the last days of her long struggle. Staring into each other's eyes, the husband and wife both knew she wouldn't last long. Their daughter knew something was wrong too. That was likely the reason why on a cold December night, after visiting her bedridden mother, the four-year-old Barbara climbed into her father's lap and broke his heart with this question: "Why isn't my mommy just like everybody else's mommy?"

Barbara felt cheated. While other children had mothers who were an active part of their lives, Barbara's mother was too sick to do anything but talk to her. Barbara couldn't remember her mother playing with her, reading her stories, or taking her for walks. To the small child, this seemed unfair.

Bob was faced with a huge dilemma. How could he explain to his daughter that her mother really did love her in ways she didn't understand? There had to be a way to provide an answer to the child.

Bob was creative. He had been making up stories since childhood. As a young boy, when other kids would pick on him, calling him names and pushing him around, Bob would retreat into a fantasy world where he was a hero. He imagined he possessed skills needed to save the day. Now, unable to provide a cure for his wife, he used his storytelling ability to address his daughter's disillusionment and change her frown to a smile.

On that windy winter's night, May made up a story about an odd-looking reindeer who lived with Santa at the North Pole. At this point, the reindeer was just small and different. His personality was part Bob and part Evelyn. Barbara loved the story and asked for it again the next night.

For more than a week, May retold the story each night. As he did, the tale grew more complex. The small reindeer was not as strong as others, and his voice was not as deep, but he had huge eyes that could see in the dark, enabling him to lead Santa even when there were no stars or moon. He became a hero in spite of his small stature and strange looks.

As May's story grew, so did his curiosity about reindeer. He even made a trip to the zoo. It was this trip, as well as seeing neon lights shining in the fog along the Lake Michigan shoreline and along Michigan Avenue, that led him to give his reindeer a red nose that acted like a fog light.

With the story nearing completion, May created a home-made book for his daughter as a Christmas present. At about this same time, his wife died. The book made the loss of her mother much easier on the child, and Barbara showed it to everyone who came to visit the family. One of those guests worked with May at Montgomery Ward. He convinced May to share his story at the company's New Year's Eve party.

May had written funny skits for past company parties, so having him perform at the event was nothing new. This time, as his story embraced a more childlike theme, many of the employees didn't know what to make of it. Some liked the tale, while others dismissed it as silly. A few believed that the corny work was the product of the pressure Bob had been under because of his wife's illness. When the night ended and the party broke up, most forgot all about the little reindeer.

However, one man was impressed enough to later call Bob into his office. Stewell Avery was the chairman of the board of Montgomery Ward. With the effect of the Depression now shrinking and sales growing, Avery was interested in coming up with a promotion for the next Christmas season. He sensed that May's story had potential. While he wasn't too excited by the reindeer angle, he offered to pay Bob a bonus of three hundred dollars if he could rework the piece into something the company could use as a giveaway during the holiday season of 1939.

Three hundred dollars was a huge sum to the cash-strapped writer, so May went to work. He refined his tale, changing the lead character's name from Rollo to Rudolph. He couldn't find a way to make the story's central focus anything but a reindeer. Intent on keeping that element, he had a friend make a new drawing of the creature. Avery gave in to the reindeer concept, and the company produced the book that became a marketing hit. In the first year, Wards gave away more than two million copies of *Rudolph the Red-Nosed Reindeer*. By the time World War II broke out, the number had grown to six million.

Wards opted to discontinue giving away the much-beloved book during World War II. Avery and others decided that the name Rudolph had such a German ring, it might appear the company was not fully supporting the war efforts. As soon as the war was over, the red-nosed reindeer came back to the company as an annual holiday giveaway item.

In the postwar boom, Avery and Wards were besieged by offers from several major publishing houses wanting to print a new version of the story. Avery had a real problem. He paid Bob May a small amount to give the book away, but if he sold the story, then there were legal ramifications that could ultimately paint the company in a bad light. The chairman decided that the prudent move was to relinquish all rights to May. A year later, the mass-market release of *Rudolph* made the Wards' copywriter a wealthy man.

With the book a worldwide best seller, numerous toy and product deals were signed. Rudolph appeared on jigsaw puzzles, socks, shoes, watches, banks, and Christmas lights. Stuffed animals of all sizes followed. Even a short cartoon was created. The little deer had become a huge business, generating millions of dollars in sales.

That's when songwriter Johnny Marks entered the picture. Bob May's second wife was Marks' sister. Even though Wards was pushing May to allow an established songwriter to pen a musical version of *Rudolph*, May chose his brother-in-law.

Marks would later say that he came up with the basic framework for the song while on a walk. Others point out that before that stroll, May had supposedly already written more than 80 percent of the lines used for lyrics. Whatever is the case, the songwriter needed only an hour to create music to accompany the words. When the song was published, only Marks' name appeared as a writer. May was given a 5 percent share of the royalties.

At first the small cut given the creator of *Rudolph* didn't seem to matter as no one wanted to record the song. No major recording artists were interested in the number. Bing Crosby passed on it, thinking it was too silly. Dinah Shore wanted a Christmas hit but was sure this song wasn't it. A host of other stars passed on the number. Hence 5 percent of nothing was still nothing.

Cowboy star Gene Autry was approached. Marks figured that Autry might be looking for a follow-up to his earlier Christmas hit, "Here Comes Santa Claus," and Gene, unlike Bing and Dinah, had children as his main audience. Autry had already discovered a song he felt would become a seasonal children's classic, called "If It Doesn't Snow This Christmas." The number about the reindeer might have remained an unopened musical gift if Autry's wife hadn't heard it. She loved the song and wanted her husband to sing it. But Autry still wasn't convinced.

On a summer day in 1949, Columbia Records booked three hours for Autry's Christmas session. The singer cut "If It Doesn't Snow This Christmas" first. He laid down the tracks for two other holiday songs. With the clock ticking and less than twenty minutes to go until someone else had the studio, Autry was sure there was simply not time to add a fourth cut. He remembered his wife's plea. Pulling out "Rudolph," he showed it to the studio musicians, who included famed guitar player and future country music star Johnny Bond, and suggested they give it a shot. The group quickly looked over the score, and everyone got into place. Because of the time constraints, they had only one chance to get the recording on tape. That one-take version would become the huge holiday hit.

Released in November, Gene Autry's "Rudolph the Red-Nosed Reindeer" went to number 1 on the charts, sold more than two million copies in its first holiday season, and earned Johnny Marks the title Songwriter of the Year. Marks didn't share the title with his brother-in-law, who had created the story and probably given him most of the lyric lines. Instead, he claimed all the credit for what was a team effort, and rode the holiday theme until his death, penning several more huge Christmas hits.

"Rudolph" became a successful television special, a movie, and the second-highest-selling holiday song of all time. The misunderstood creature that Bob May conjured up for his four-year-old daughter has become one of the most recognized elements of the Christmas season.

Bob May lived long enough to understand that a tough childhood and his wife's short life inspired a creature who lights up the world in a dynamic and special way. Written for a single child, the story that became a song has touched tens of millions with the lesson that we are all created for something special. As long as there is Christmas, Rudolph's unique example will continue to light the way for children everywhere.

FROSTY THE SNOWMAN

*O*nly Christmas could produce a song that has been recorded by Bing Crosby, Michael Jackson, Dr. John, the Beach Boys, the Ronettes, Roy Rogers, the Ray Conniff Orchestra, and Alvin and the Chipmunks — and has nothing to do with Christmas! In 1949, Gene Autry scored a huge hit with "Rudolph the Red-Nosed Reindeer." The song, penned by songwriter Johnny Marks and *Rudolph the Red-Nosed Reindeer* book creator Bob May, quickly became an industry success. Beyond the books and records, product lines including clothing, plush animals, and glassware abounded. The reindeer was everywhere and generating millions of dollars in sales. Songwriters were trying to marry cute creatures with all things Christmas.

Jack Rollins and Steve Nelson were intent on cashing in on the holiday concept. Rollins had scored some minor hits with country acts. Autry was familiar with his work, so Rollins and Nelson had somewhat of an inside track to the hot Christmas hit producer. Their first idea was not to land the next Yuletide novelty song. Instead, they looked to another holiday that was not nearly as commercialized.

Using a character invented by famed children's author Thornton Burgess, the musical scribes penned the Easter song "Here Comes Peter Cottontail" and submitted it to Autry. The singing cowboy, realizing money could be made beyond Easter baskets and bonnets, cut the song at the height of "Rudolph" mania, and the song released a few months after the reindeer had fallen off the charts. At any other time, "Here Comes Peter Cottontail" would have been nothing more than a children's favorite, but thanks to the trail blazed by "Rudolph" and by Autry's standing with radio disc jockeys and children, the rabbit hopped his way to number 5 on *Billboard*'s list, and Autry suddenly ranked behind only Bing Crosby as the top musical pitchman for holidays.

Autry, whose days as a country singer were waning, sensed the potential of his new role as Santa's holiday partner and looked for another Christmas song. He had scored with two titles that revolved around the adventures of the jolly old elf. The first, "Here Comes Santa Claus," served as a career revival. The second, "Rudolph," elevated him back to top-star status. With few interested in his western music, he had to score another hit to keep the momentum going. Finding that new hit became his goal for 1950.

Autry was an extremely shrewd businessman. He understood that he needed something that had the charismatic charm of his previous hits but could stand alone as a release.

Thanks to "Peter Cottontail," Nelson and Rollins now had even more of an inside track to Autry. A host of others, including Johnny Marks, wanted his next Christmas recording as well. Thus, Autry was peppered with demo records. Few were original ideas. Most were rehashes of the singing cowboy's first two hits. Some even attempted to move the Easter rabbit to Christmas and have him join forces with Rudolph and Santa.

Nelson and Rollins worked on the Christmas concept for months. Everything the pair created so far didn't have any real "zing." Only after Nelson and Rollins stepped away from the holiday and turned their attention to other assignments was a creative Christmas idea born.

To most Americans, Christmas was not Christmas without snow. Kids looked forward to the cold, fluffy white so they could play and build snowmen. The songwriters latched onto this concept and then asked a question that Walt Disney would have appreciated: what if a snowman could come to life? What if the children could construct a best friend?

In a child's imagination, anything is possible. Why not take a snowman and make him almost human? The songwriters needed a storyline. They couldn't just start with a living snowman. What would bring him to life? A hat filled with magic.

Once they developed a concept, the song came together. When the singing cowboy heard "Frosty the Snowman," one feature made the demo record stand out: the song was not directly tied to Christmas. It was more than just a holiday number. Autry took great care with this new recording. "Rudolph" had been recorded quickly, with little thought to the song having lasting appeal, but "Frosty the Snowman" was carefully arranged and prepared. Columbia brought in Carl Cotner's Orchestra for the music and the Cass County Boys for backup vocals. Every facet of the recording was monitored to assure quality. After all, Autry's new cut was following in the hoofprints of a legend.

Insiders at the record label felt that releasing "Frosty the Snowman" during Rudolph's second year would be a mistake. They believed that the song might be overshadowed or even buried by the reindeer. Some believed it would be best to hold the snowman back until 1951, but the urge to cash in on the holidays was simply too strong to resist. The song about the snowman was released in late November.

"Frosty" jumped onto the charts a week after "Rudolph," on December 9. The song's whimsical story and catchy tune caught on and even affected the American language. Building a snowman became known as creating a "Frosty." Because of the record, old top hats were taken out of trunks and placed on the heads of snowmen. While the singing snowman didn't rise as high as the flying reindeer, the song cracked the top 10 by Christmas Day.

As with Rudolph, Frosty's marketing potential was not missed by those in the business world. One of the first to jump on the bandwagon was Little Golden Books. Then a decade old, Golden Books were a staple of every child's life. Beginning with *Three Little Kittens*, these small children's publications had exploded as a giant in the children's product industry. Working with Nelson and Rollins, the company created a best seller with the book version of "Frosty the Snowman." Toys, a cartoon, and comics followed.

Since being cut by Gene Autry, "Frosty the Snowman" has been recorded by hundreds of artists. Red Foley, Nat King Cole, Ella Fitzgerald, Leon Redbone, and child sensation Connie Talbot have all put their stamp on the number. In 1969, with Jackie Vernon supplying the voice of Frosty, it was spun off into a hit CBS television special. This expanded version of the snowman story, complete with a villain and heroic children, has been seen on television every Christmas since.

Why did "Frosty the Snowman" work? Why did this song make it when hundreds of others failed? The talent and timing of Gene Autry. "Frosty the Snowman" was the final Christmas hit for the singing cowboy. If Autry had cut it four years later, after his star had waned, Frosty might have simply melted away.

The song also survived because of something that Steve Nelson and Jack Rollins built into it. Frosty was created out of the fun elements of holidays. Snow is something that children of all ages love to play in. The songwriters delivered a bright, magical promise of hope and fun. Even as he melted, Frosty assured his friends that he would be back again. Just like Christmas, Frosty returns to delight us every year.

SILVER BELLS

S ilver Bells" should have been a huge hit for Bob Hope, but when it came to Christmas, Bob was always left out in the cold, while Bing Crosby's home was kept warm by royalty checks generated from seasonal record sales.

In 1950, Hope was given a role in a movie based on a beloved Damon Runyon short story. The film was a remake of two 1934 movies, *The Lemon Drop Kid*, starring fast-talking Lee Tracy, and Shirley Temple's *Little Miss Marker*, which were based on the same story.

Hope used music in most of his films. These numbers were then reused by Hope on his radio show to help promote the release of his movies. Two years before the actor began work on the Runyon tale, a pair of Jewish songwriters had successfully penned some wonderful songs for Hope's western comedy *The Paleface*. Because of their extraordinary work in that film, Jay Livingston and Ray Evans were assigned to write three songs for *The Lemon Drop Kid*. One of the numbers needed to embrace a Christmas theme.

Livingston and Evans had been working together for several years and had recently penned the incredibly popular "Mona Lisa." Thus, the pair was hot, and everybody was beating on their door, hoping to take a look at their latest compositions. It is hardly surprising that Paramount Pictures sought them out to write the music for *The Lemon Drop Kid*.

As they read the script, Livingston and Evans found themselves with a unique challenge. Scores of movies had been set at Christmas, and almost as many holiday songs had been written for those films. Yet none used a city for their principle locations. Thus, this would be the first time an urban area would be the backdrop for a Christmas number. How could the songwriting duo recast the image of the holiday — one associated with forests, rural homes, and sleigh rides — in a song set on the streets of New York?

The songwriters brainstormed in Evans' office. As they ran through Runyon's story, they discovered a bit of inspiration. At one point in the movie, Hope's character stands on a corner dressed as Santa and ringing a bell. This prompted the men to discuss all the bells that ring in the city during the holidays — bells on the horses in Central Park, church bells, and Salvation Army bells. But what else defined the holidays? The writers hit on the answer: the colors of Christmas.

In those days, most stoplights were only red or green. Those were also the colors most associated with Christmas. Every traffic signal in New York was blinking out in celebration of the holiday.

The rest of the images needed for the song came easily. Livingston and Evans knew they needed to work into their lyrics the bustle of shoppers and the images of decorated stores.

Marilyn Maxwell, an actress who had solid vocal skills, would be costarring with Hope. In the scene where the Christmas song was to be used, the pair would be walking down the street. With the lyrics in place, the men put together a melody and an arrangement for a duet.

After they finished the Christmas song, they went over to Evans' home and played it for his wife. The men were shocked when she almost fell off the couch laughing at what they viewed as a sentimental look at the holidays. When she was finally able to compose herself, she asked if the men knew there were two meanings to the word *tinkle* — and one had nothing to do with bells!

The men shook their heads.

She then explained it was what many mothers had their children say when they needed to go to the bathroom. She was concerned that with a song called "Tinkle Bell," audiences would think more of bathrooms than of Christmas, and so they decided on "Silver Bells."

Hope and Maxwell had just the right amount of sentiment combined with an easygoing pacing. Though it was filmed on a Hollywood back lot, the scene where they performed had all the elements of a New York Christmas, including snow, shoppers, and red and green stoplights. With *The Lemon Drop Kid* not scheduled for release until March of the following year,

"Silver Bells" would have remained completely unknown during the 1950 holiday season if not for Hope's good friend Bing Crosby.

In fifteen years since he scored a hit with "Silent Night," Crosby had amassed more holiday record sales than anyone in history. His voice was featured on everything from traditional carols to the most beloved secular holiday tunes. Thus, he was always on the prowl for a new Christmas standard he could introduce.

Crosby agreed that "Silver Bells" was best presented as a duet. He contacted a radio singer named Carol Richards and offered her a chance to record it with him. His choice of Richards was ironic, as the Illinois native had been brought to Hollywood upon winning a talent search hosted by Bob Hope. Crosby had Hope's talent discovery in a studio to record a song written for Hope.

The marriage of Crosby's and Richards' voices made for a powerful record. Released in October 1950, the song became Crosby's third-most popular holiday hit. The single's success prompted Paramount Studios to take another look at the way "Silver Bells" had been filmed in *The Lemon Drop Kid*. Hope and Maxwell were called back to the studio six months after their film had wrapped, and the duet was reshot with a much more elaborate backdrop. Although the movie was released three months after Christmas, publicity emphasized that "Silver Bells" was included in the musical score. Perhaps because audiences were confused as to why a movie that was set at Christmas was released in March,

The Lemon Drop Kid was not a smash hit. Today, this entertaining film is mainly remembered as giving Hope a chance to sing "Silver Bells."

Though he failed to get the hit recording with the Christmas song written for him, Hope owned the holiday in another way. Starting in 1942 and continuing for two generations, the Hollywood star gave up his Christmases to entertain men and women in uniform all over the globe. While he may have dressed up as Santa in *The Lemon Drop Kid*, on these entertainment junkets, even without the red costume, he became Santa to millions of lonely servicemen and servicewomen. On each of these visits, Hope sang "Silver Bells" for the audiences. For more than four decades, his voice and that song brought each listener a bit closer to home.

The first successful song written about Christmas in the city may have initially had a funny title, but the sentiment and imagery found in its final lyrics continue to touch millions of hearts each year.

I Saw Mommy Kissing
Santa Claus

uring World War II, Tommie Connor penned an English holiday song that deeply touched those fighting the Nazis. Though almost completely unknown in America, Connor's "I'm Sending a Letter to Santa" was a sentimental hit in the writer's homeland. The song might have remained Connor's signature piece if he had not stumbled upon a certain humorous image in a magazine.

Almost everyone who glanced at the holiday advertisement saw the image for what it was — a father and mother trying to make sure that if their children were spying on events in the living room, they would catch a glimpse of a man in a red suit and not Daddy. This charade had been a part of Christmas for years. But Connor wondered: what if the woman was so overcome by the moment that she kissed Santa? The act was innocent, since she was kissing her own husband. But what if the children didn't know it was their daddy in the Santa suit? What would the children think?

The idea was the perfect holiday mix of tradition coupled

with misunderstanding, with a subtle touch of naughty thrown in. To be something other than a ribald, almost off-color pub number, the song had to poke fun and express shock without being too wicked. Connor decided to make the narrator a child. When Connor finished his work, he felt he had conveyed his idea in a way acceptable to everyone. He soon discovered this was not the case.

The image that inspired Connor was from the ad department at the Nieman Marcus Department Store Company. In the wholesome environment of the early 1950s, the image was meant to bring a bit of adult humor into a childhood holiday and would have been forgotten if Connor had not framed it with words and music.

When given the demo record, Columbia Records' CEO Mitch Miller liked Connor's "I Saw Mommy Kissing Santa Claus." He knew the perfect child singer: Jimmy Boyd. Boyd had grown up living the story portrayed in the best-selling book and award-winning 1939 movie *The Grapes of Wrath*. Born in Mississippi the same year the film was released, his family was so poor that they used their life savings for train fare to California. With no money for food or shelter, the Boyds often ate in soup kitchens and lived in abandoned shacks. Christmas was just like any other day, as the parents had no money for presents.

Though the family had little money and few prospects, they did have a number of hand-me-down and homemade instruments. Thus, to bring a bit of joy to their lives and pass the time, they sat under trees and played old folk songs. As people in the area heard the Boyds' informal outdoor concerts, word got around that they had a unique gift. Beginning with local dances, the family soon was making some much-needed added income as entertainers.

In 1947, the family band performed at a Colton, California, barn dance where Jimmy sang a few songs and did a bit of guitar picking. The crowd loved the freckle-faced kid. Within two weeks, Boyd was being featured on the radio. His weekly take of fifty dollars was more than the family often made in a month. In a sense, the eight-year-old had put them in high cotton for the first time in their lives.

Within three years of the barn dance, the child caught the attention of a new medium — television. Betty White introduced Boyd to Los Angeles audiences on her program *Hollywood on Television*. Scores of appearances followed. By the early 1950s, the preteen had established himself as a local star. Blessed with an inflective country voice, a toothy smile, and charm, Boyd possessed the exact traits Mitch Miller felt were needed to sing "I Saw Mommy Kissing Santa Claus."

In 1952, Columbia signed Boyd to a recording contract and brought the twelve-year-old into the Los Angeles studio to record Connor's song. Little time was taken in the session. As Miller was looking for a raw, almost unprofessional sound, the producer didn't spend much time polishing the final product. The boy learned the music, and the session players backed him up. The record was shipped in late November. Miller was confident the song would appear on the charts, though he expected nothing more — and if some of the best-known moral voices in America had not gotten involved, "I Saw Mommy Kissing Santa Claus" likely would have remained a moderate hit.

Within a week of its release, the Archdiocese of Boston condemned "I Saw Mommy Kissing Santa Claus" as immoral. Other groups from both the Catholic and Protestant churches followed suit. Missing the point that the man in the lyrics was actually a husband dressed up like Santa, people wrote articles and gave speeches deriding the song for casting Old St. Nick as a man who played around on the side. Hundreds argued this song was sending a horrible message to America's innocent children.

Miller sensed that Boyd's record might get banned everywhere if something was not done. The producer also realized that the negative press was generating a great deal of free publicity and interest. He needed to walk a fine line to calm the hysterical voices and save the reputation of his record company and still cash in on the press. The label decided to put Boyd on a plane and fly the boy across the country to meet with the head of the Catholic Church in Boston. Cameras were on hand as the child explained to the church leader the song's real punch line. This was not an affair — it was a father making the season magic for his children. His wife was so overcome by her husband's generous and loving actions that she felt the need to thank him with a kiss. Thanks to Boyd's well-rehearsed explanation, the church took a second look at the song and removed its objections. In the process, millions tuned in to hear what all the fuss was about.

Thanks in no small part to the noise made by Catholic and Protestant church leaders, Boyd's "I Saw Mommy Kissing Santa Claus" quickly jumped to number 1 and stayed there for two weeks. Miller was so thrilled, he immediately began looking for another novelty number for his child prodigy. Meanwhile, with childlike modestly, Boyd told *Time* magazine, "I like it personally, but I didn't think anyone would buy it." Within a year, three million records were sold.

Thanks to the holiday song, Boyd became an international sensation for a few years. He cut several more records, starring in movies and on television. Though Boyd worked in entertainment the remainder of his life, he never really escaped the song's shadow. As much as the song brought him fame and fortune, it also trapped him. Even in his fifties, when he worked local fairs, he would be introduced as the kid who sang the Christmas novelty number.

When Tommie Connor penned "I Saw Mommy Kissing Santa Claus," he knew his song had a great hook. The lyrics framed an image that was both sweet and naughty. What he couldn't have guessed was that his secular composition would owe its success to the influence of the Catholic Church. Thanks to being banned, "I Saw Mommy Kissing Santa Claus" gained the exposure needed to make Jimmy Boyd forever young and his song an annual holiday treat.

CAROLING, CAROLING

ome artists' work isn't treasured until after they die. These artists never realize the scope of their creation or the number of people impacted by their work. Other artists die and their creation dies with them. A few artists have champions, someone who loves that artist and works to ensure that their contributions aren't lost nor their talents forgotten. Alfred Burt's wife and friends would not allow his work to die after cancer claimed his life. They kept knocking on doors until someone answered.

Without a series of simple, homemade Christmas cards, none of Alfred Burt's work would have been saved. In 1922, Father Bates Burt grew tired of sending out generic holiday greetings. While the cards he ordered were beautiful and had touching messages, everyone bought the same ones. The Episcopal priest hatched a new plan. He composed an original Christmas poem, wrote music, and had the song printed on a holiday card. He continued this practice for the next two decades as his card list grew from fifty to hundreds.

Bates was not a trained musician, so when his son,

Alfred, showed signs of musical talent, the priest enrolled him in music lessons. Alfred played at church and in school. He worked with local kids to develop fresh arrangements of songs for dances. Determined to make his mark in the world of entertainment, the younger Burt majored in music at the University of Michigan, where he was often the college band's featured trumpeter. He probably would have headed to New York to audition with big bands if World War II had not interrupted his plans. Drafted into the military, the young man was spending his last weeks at home when his father asked him to pen the music for the family's twentieth-anniversary Christmas card.

The father estimated that the son would provide a song in just a few days. Concerned with going to war, Alfred took more than a month to complete "O, Christmas Cometh Caroling." But it was worth the wait.

While the elder Burt loved carols that rang with pomp and circumstance, Alfred preferred jazz. For the first time, the family Christmas card reflected the rhythm and style of American pop music. In the midst of a war, this upbeat carol was widely embraced by many of the five hundred who were now on the family's mailing list. Neither father nor son guessed the song would forever link the Burt name to popular Christmas music.

During the four years Burt was away serving his country, he composed the music for his father's cards. After the war, Alfred worked with various bands and toured the country. By the early fifties, television was taking off, and Burt moved to Los Angeles to arrange music for variety shows. In his early thirties, a new father with a blossoming career, Burt seemed to have the world by the tail. Then tragedy hit. A persistent cough led him to seek medical help. Burt was dying of cancer.

His life was over before it really began. The Broadway musical he had planned would not be written, and he would never compose a chart-topping single, score a motion picture, or watch his daughter grow up.

Just after Thanksgiving, the Blue Reys, a nationally known singing group, opened one of Burt's Christmas cards. The group loved "Come, Dear Children" and performed it on the annual King Sisters' TV Christmas show. James Conkling, the president of Columbia Records, heard the performance. Conkling wanted to find out who wrote the song. At their meeting, Burt handed the recording giant's president a decade's worth of his original Christmas cards. After studying them, Conkling asked Burt if the songwriter could pen four more songs so Columbia could produce an album of nothing but Alfred Burt Christmas carols.

Encouraged by his wife, Anne, the weakened composer went to work. From his wheelchair, barely able to whisper, he pushed himself to write. As he finished melody lines, he sent them to Wihla Huston, a church organist who had known him since childhood. Working against a deadline made even tighter because of Burt's precarious health, Huston created for one of the melodies a poem that reflected something she remembered of Burt's youth. He had caroled with other kids from his father's church. On those winter outings, Burt was the life of the party. Huston recalled those moments in bright, upbeat verses. When he received Huston's "Caroling, Caroling," Burt needed only a few hours to complete the arrangement.

Just before Christmas, 1953, with all four new songs finished, a volunteer chorus organized by the King Sisters, Buddy Cole, and Jimmy Joyce met in a North Hollywood church to do the initial taping for the album. Burt managed to make it to the church. When he heard "Caroling, Caroling," it was almost as if he had been healed. His face lit up and his eyes came alive.

According to his daughter, Diane, later that night Burt told his wife, "This is the happiest day of my life." Time was running out for the songwriter. Within a month and a half, his final work completed, Burt died. His last request was that Anne care for their daughter and his music. She proved ready for both jobs.

Though the album's release was a flop, Anne refused to give up. For the next eight years, she played her late husband's carols for anyone who would listen. The first act that signed on was Tennessee Ernie Ford. The popular television host recorded Burt's "The Star Carol." The single rocketed onto the charts and peaked at number 4. Despite the success, no one wanted to record another of Burt's songs. Finally, arranger and songwriter Ralph Carmichael discovered the out-of-print Columbia album featuring all of Burt's carols and noted a song with potential.

Nat King Cole, an artist who had all but defined the season with "The Christmas Song," was recording a new holiday album. Every songwriter in town was trying to land a song on his release. Confident he had the perfect number for Cole's smooth baritone voice, Carmichael took "Caroling, Caroling" to Cole's producer. A hopeful Carmichael barely got in the front door before being told that Cole wanted to cut only traditional carols. No new songs were needed. Carmichael was heartbroken. He had practically assured Anne Burt he could place "Caroling, Caroling" with Cole. What was he going to tell her?

When Carmichael turned to make his exit, Cole walked in. The singer and arranger visited for a few minutes, and Carmichael pitched Burt's holiday song. Cole probably had little interest in hearing the number, but the sad story of Burt's untimely death touched his heart. Rather than simply dismiss the song, he found a record player and took a listen. As the demo played, Cole first smiled and then laughed. "Caroling, Caroling" found a place on his new album. The final rendition was smooth and warm, like a good cup of hot chocolate. You could almost hear the singer's smiles as he shaped the lyrics with his voice.

Cole's version of "Caroling, Caroling" was an immediate hit and became an annual Christmas tradition on radio stations around the world. In a miracle of modern production, Natalie Cole cut Burt's holiday classic as a duet with her father long after he had died of cancer. That version is almost as popular as Nat King Cole's original. Now recorded by hundreds of different artists and groups, "Caroling, Caroling" sparked a deep interest in Burt's other carols. Artists as varied as James Taylor, Simon and Garfunkel, and the Boston Pops Orchestra have recorded Burt's holiday songs.

Anne Burt's happy marriage lasted just over ten years. When her husband died, she held his hand and promised to watch over his legacy. Promoting his carols when few were interested, she kept knocking on doors until someone answered. A man who never quite got to the top of his profession during his lifetime emerged as one of the composing giants of holiday music. Thanks to a family tradition of homemade Christmas cards, the world has been blessed with "Caroling, Caroling."

IT'S BEGINNING TO LOOK
A LOT LIKE CHRISTMAS

*R*eplayed thousands of times during each new holiday season, "It's Beginning to Look a Lot Like Christmas" seems to be one of those songs destined to become a classic from the start. Yet this ode to the holiday stumbled out of the gates, not finding its footing for almost a year. When it caught on, "It's Beginning to Look a Lot Like Christmas" became almost as vital to the holiday season as the myriad of traditions its lyrics celebrate.

The Christmas classic was born in the fertile imagination of Meredith Wilson, but unlike many of his timeless hits, this one would be triggered by the work of another band of artists. It took that group, put together by the legendary movie producer Darryl Zanuck, to jump-start the songwriter's creative juices and put Wilson into a holiday frame of mind. In other words, it took being at the right place at the right time, and that seemed to be the story of Wilson's life.

Wilson was a musical prodigy as a child, playing a host of instruments and composing tunes even before learning to read. He migrated from the farmlands of Iowa to the Big Apple as a teen, studying at the Juilliard School of Music and then playing in the famed John Philip Sousa's marching band. He was in his early twenties when he began a stint with the New York Philharmonic Orchestra and nearing thirty when he packed his bags and moved to California to work in radio. A few years later he landed in Hollywood, where he penned songs for movies such as *The Great Dictator* and *The Little Foxes*. By 1940, almost everyone in the music business knew his name.

Like millions of others, Wilson served in the military during World War II. Unlike those whose wartime service left them out in the cold, the songwriter found the doors of Hollywood open to him in 1945. Over the next two years, he composed classics including "You and I," "May the Good Lord Bless and Keep You," and "Till There Was You." He was on top of the world and a source of envy among songwriters, but in the midst of great success he was also bored. Though the motion pictures offered him more work than he could handle, he hungered for new challenges. Leaving security behind, he moved across the country to give the entertainment mecca he had not conquered a shot.

For Wilson, Broadway — known by actors and producers as the Great White Way — offered a chance to push his creativity in a new direction. Unlike others who had failed in New York, he found almost instant success and acceptance. During the fifties and sixties, he all but owned Times Square as musicals such as *The Unsinkable Molly Brown* and

The Music Man revealed that he was one of those rare individuals who could write music for any stage or venue.

In the summer of 1947, Wilson followed in the steps of many Americans to watch a new movie being marketed as a love story. Shot on location in New York at many of the same places Wilson now saw every day, *Miracle on 34th Street* was a film Hollywood really didn't believe in. Though it was set at Christmas and dealt with Santa Claus, Twentieth Century Fox Studios tried to hide those details in its marketing campaign. Instead of focusing on the holiday, they played up a love story between a store employee and a lonely man. Within days of its release, that angle had been completely forgotten as the nation was awash in the glow of a Christmas in June, July, and August. The film's draw was so strong, the movie was still luring fans into theaters six months after it came out.

Wilson was charmed by the tale of a young girl coming to believe in the magic of Santa. Rather than just embrace the emotions of the moment, he went back to his office and began to jot down ideas to turn the movie into a Broadway musical. He felt that music could bring this New York tale to life in a way that the drama of a motion picture could not. Beyond composing a couple of numbers, Wilson didn't get far on his concept. It was soon placed on the back burner as he worked on the shows that would make him the toast of the Big Apple.

A couple of years later, while staying in Yarmouth, Nova Scotia, Wilson must have again thought of *Miracle on 34th*

Street. In this Canadian town, Christmas seemed to be every-where — in the lobby of the Grand Hotel, at the community tree, and in the store window displays. No one knows for sure if this was the trigger to his inspiration, but within a few months Wilson created a magical number that spoke not just of those locations but also of the other wonderful elements of the holiday that make it so special.

When its lyric lines are studied in detail, "It's Beginning to Look a Lot Like Christmas" seems almost a musical ver-sion of a Norman Rockwell painting. The song is bursting with images, one right after another, that create a visual feast of Christmas pictures. In a little more than three minutes' worth of words, Wilson managed to squeeze all the toys, emotions, scenes, and even smells of the holiday. In spite of its seemingly overcrowded and wordy lines, the song's pacing is as smooth and unhurried as a sleigh ride across Central Park. The work was perfectly tied up when Wilson added a scene of home and family.

One of the first to hear Wilson's composition was the seventh son of a seventh son. Perry Como latched onto this magical piece in September 1951. Using the Fontane Sisters for backup and employing Mitchell Ayres and His Orchestra, Como brought Wilson's holiday number to life in an RCA stu-dio. The crooner's easy pacing and smooth approach fit the carol like a well-worn leather glove. The final result seemed perfectly suited for the audience of the time. Almost everyone in the studio felt they would be rewarded with a big holiday hit. Como, one of the big stars of his day, wasn't so sure.

Como had been a singing barber into his early twenties. In 1933, his patrons encouraged him to hang up his clippers and audition with the Freddy Carlone band. He landed a gig, and for the next decade Como toured the nation, copying the style of his idol Bing Crosby to the point of singing many of Crosby's hits. During this time, not one record company offered him a contract. Though he had a fun ride, he felt he was a failure as an entertainer. His pockets were empty and his options few. He was in the process of renting a barbershop and picking up his clippers when CBS gave him a chance to host a radio show. Now that his voice was heard each week from coast to coast, RCA called with a recording offer. Almost overnight, Como had a monster hit, "Till the End of Time," and became a household name. Sensing the potential of a new medium, in 1948 Como became one of the first recording stars to jump to television. He was hosting his successful program when he released "It's Beginning to Look a Lot Like Christmas."

A month after the singing barber cut "It's Beginning to Look a Lot Like Christmas," Bing Crosby recorded his own version of Wilson's tune. Both records were released within days of each other, but neither made much of a splash. Not until 1952 did Como's rerelease of Wilson's Christmas ballad break onto the *Billboard* charts and jump into the top 20. For the next generation, millions felt it simply wasn't Christmas until they tuned into Como's holiday show and heard him sing "It's Beginning to Look a Lot Like Christmas."

For four decades, Wilson's holiday offering remained

Perry Como's signature song. Still, that didn't keep others from trying to make "It's Beginning to Look a Lot Like Christmas" their own. In 1986, Johnny Mathis recorded it, and six years later it became a Mathis hit when it was used in *Home Alone 2*. Most recently, Connie Talbot, a child singer who rocked the program *Britain's Got Talent,* generated huge European sales with her spin on Wilson's now six-decade-old classic.

"It's Beginning to Look a Lot Like Christmas" probably did more to capture the real joy of an American Christmas than any other popular holiday standard. The song is as warm and inviting as a fire and as friendly as Santa's smile. Like the timeless movie that inspired it, "It's Beginning to Look a Lot Like Christmas" reminds listeners that the holidays are a series of special moments woven together into a quilt of love and wonder that covers us with the pure and unequalled joy of Christmas.

(THERE'S NO PLACE LIKE) HOME FOR THE HOLIDAYS

P erry Como was the perfect radio and television host. His easygoing style, sincere expression, upbeat, gentle voice, and steady mannerisms drew mass audiences. Como was the guy next door, the favorite uncle or brother, the man everyone liked and trusted.

Como started his adult life as a barber, which helped him develop a knack for putting people at ease. He had a gift for connecting one-to-one. Perhaps no one ever to host a television show was better at this than the Singing Barber. The millions who tuned in to his shows each week felt as if Como were performing just for them. Como made his fans feel like friends.

Como was the Mr. Rogers of adult programming. He created a place on television where adults could relax. He never challenged anyone, but welcomed them to his home on the air. This was especially true at Christmas, when he brought out the holiday decorations and performed with great sincerity the most beloved songs of the season.

For many, Como was a real part of their family during Christmas.

In 1954, Como was celebrating his sixth year on television. He had already scored a major holiday hit with "It's Beginning to Look a Lot Like Christmas" but wanted to add something new for this holiday season. Rather than go through a stack of demo recordings of fresh seasonal tunes, Como turned to two of his most trusted friends and asked them to create something original. He didn't want another generic Christmas song; he wanted a song that reflected *his* view of the season.

For several years, Al Stillman and Robert Allen had worked as music arrangers for Como's televised variety program. They had even come together to pen several of his hits. They weren't surprised when Como presented them with his new challenge.

Stillman was closing in on fifty, a former newspaper reporter who landed in show business as a writer for Radio City Music Hall. By the time Como asked him to come up with a new set of Christmas songs, Stillman had composed the lyrics for more than fifty hits. Though he could write any style, he was especially drawn to ballads.

Allen was only in his late twenties when Como signed him as a pianist and arranger. He not only was a force behind the scenes on the television show but also was often seen in front of the camera, tickling the ivories as the host sang. Besides his work for his boss, Allen had also penned the music to a number of classic songs, including Johnny

Mathis's classic "Chances Are." Como knew he had a solid team working on his Christmas song wish list.

At this point in his career, Como ranked with Nat King Cole and just behind Bing Crosby as the world's top holiday vocalist. Each year, his Christmas records were played on the radio and purchased by the thousands for personal enjoyment and as gifts. RCA wanted a series of new, fresh recordings in order to cash in on the holiday rush for Como's music. The two writers were feeling the pressure not just to compose something new for the variety show but also to create music that would generate radio play and sales. They were asked to merge Como's personality with fan expectations and a record label's desires, but this was just the beginning of the writers' complicated task.

Como was a deeply spiritual man who loved to sing traditional carols. To him, Christmas was both a time for gathering with friends and family and a time for worship and praise. The writers knew that the album had to contain a few spiritual holiday numbers arranged in the singer's style. Yet RCA didn't want to push a single that was religious; they wanted one that reflected the upbeat nature of the holidays. The writers knew that their boss was not looking for something as light as "Rudolph" or "Frosty," but the label didn't want to release a new version of "O Come, All Ye Faithful" or "O Holy Night." What was in between?

Stillman, whose Jewish faith gave him a unique perspective on an American Christmas, saw the holidays as a time when family gathered to renew the bonds of love and fellowship. In the days before commercial airline travel and at a time when almost all major roads were two-lane black-top, getting home for Christmas was not easy. Meanwhile, the Great Depression and World War II had spread many families out, literally from coast to coast. The Herculean task of getting home set the stage for the writer's lyrics. With these thoughts in mind, Stillman went to work. Rather than using the word *Christmas*, he opted to embrace the line "There's no place like home for the holidays." This set in motion a concept that quickly fell into verse.

Though universal in nature, the song had a rural feel. Stillman's lyrical genius was placing these images on full display while coupling them with the perils of travel. His words included traffic jams, the taste of homemade pumpkin pie, the warmth seen in a friendly face, and the soothing melody of a doorbell signaling the end of a long trip.

Allen took Stillman's lyrics and built a musical platform to fit Como's relaxed, warm vocal style. Though never rushed, the song's arrangement carried listeners quickly along on the trip to the magical place called home. Ultimately, thanks to the perfect marriage of words and music, the song was so personal that anyone could claim it as their own.

Though it was the last song written in an all-day session and not the writers' favorite, Como picked "Home for the Holidays" as the winner. He recorded the song a week before Thanksgiving, and the single raced up to number 8 before Christmas. The Como classic reappeared on the charts again for several more years.

While "Home for the Holidays" was a hit at record outlets, it was an even bigger hit on television. For millions, the song defined the way they saw Perry Como and Christmas. He gave voice to their holiday. Watching him perform on his show, audiences felt as if they were being invited into his home. Like few others, Como had reached fans' hearts.

"Home for the Holidays" has since been cut by scores of artists, but it remains Perry Como's song. This is due in no small part to the fact that Al Stillman and Robert Allen wrote it for the singer. Thus, it is unique in Christmas lore. Only a few holiday songs have ever been written with a single artist in mind. "Home for the Holidays" ranks behind only Bing Crosby's "White Christmas" in this special category, and no song has better reflected its singer's personality than Como's warm, sincere carol.

20

BLUE CHRISTMAS

lue Christmas" was penned by a man known mainly for writing now-forgotten commercial radio jingles and was recorded by a former truck driver from Memphis. While Elvis Presley is best remembered in December for this rock-and-roll hit, the Christmas song he most deeply treasured was one he cut in the sixties titled "If Every Day Was Just Like Christmas." He recorded the latter hoping this sentimental number would become his signature holiday piece. However, even though "Every Day" hit the charts and remains a beloved recording, it simply couldn't escape the giant shadow of "Blue Christmas," which emerged as a rocking holiday hit because of Presley's love of country music.

Elvis Presley was eclectic in his musical taste. The King of Rock and Roll loved crooners like Frank Sinatra, Tony Bennett, and Dean Martin. He was also drawn to music from the Memphis blues community. He dreamed of being a part of gospel groups such as the Blackwood Brothers, the Stamps Quartet, and the Statesmen. His introduction to "Blue Christmas" came via a man who preferred a different sound. Ernest Tubb, known affectionately as the Texas Troubadour, captured the first hit version of "Blue Christmas." This hillbilly classic, released in 1949, hit number 1 on the country charts and became the genre's first Christmas hit. Until Tubb cut it, the song had been all but dismissed as a minor holiday offering. Without Tubb, Elvis, who was also a big country music fan, would have never heard the song, but the tune's journey to Elvis status began years earlier.

Jay Johnson developed the idea for "Blue Christmas" while commuting from his home in Stamford, Connecticut, to his job in New York City. The trip always began with Johnson jumping into the front seat of his well-worn 1939 Mercury and racing to a train station. On this early winter morning, a cold rain was falling in buckets, and, as his car's top had a large gash over the driver's seat, Johnson was forced to pop an umbrella through the roof to keep the rain off his head. Johnson was soggy and blue.

At forty-five, Johnson had labored in obscurity. He dreamed of penning a script for an award-winning radio show or composing a hit for one of the nation's top crooners but instead made his living writing advertising jingles and scripts for local radio. He had a briefcase filled with these ideas, but other than his family, few saw any promise in Johnson's labors. Even in the face of constant rejection, and even though he was working with the knowledge that no one really heard his best ideas, the middle-aged man refused to give up. Each day as he rode the commuter train, he scribbled down ideas he believed he could turn into something the postwar public would love. Songs like "Peaceful," "Wedding Bells," "Telephone Fever," "Sunday Afternoon," and "Peter Pan the Meter Man" didn't generate much interest with publishers or recording artists. On this rainy day, an idea came to him that would eventually place Johnson in the unofficial Holiday Hall of Fame.

Johnson was assigned to write a script for a radio show that embraced the music of the season. As he thought about all the seasonal classics, he realized that many people were sad at Christmas. They were alone, heartsick, and awash in depression. For them, the holidays weren't white but blue. With blues music a national sensation, why not write a song about a blue Christmas? As the commuter train roared down the tracks, with rain beating on the windows, Johnson wrote the initial verse of what would become his only national hit composition.

Several days later, Johnson fleshed out "Blue Christmas." In the process, he scrapped those first four lines, as well as scores of others. The final lyrics were for those who didn't have a loved one to share the merriest days of the year, those who didn't have gifts under the tree, those who lacked hope for a bright new year. Not exactly the classic cheery Christmas theme!

Once Johnson completed the lyrics, he teamed up with composer Billy Hayes. "Blue Christmas" became the mournful opposite of almost every other holiday song ever written. Even though the song's subject was anything but merry, Choice Music gave Johnson and Hayes an advance for publishing rights. Hugo Winterhalter and His Orchestra recorded the tune.

Columbia Records thought "Blue Christmas" would land their new star in the top 10. They were right. The song reached number 9. The following Christmas, it reappeared on the pop charts.

Ernest Tubb, a country music star who specialized in Texas honky-tonk music, heard Winterhalter's release in 1948. He immediately worked the song into his act. Buoyed by requests from his fans, a year later he cut the number for Decca Records. The Christmas release became Tubb's fourth number 1 recording and his twenty-ninth top 40 hit in just four years. For the rest of his life, "Blue Christmas" would be the Country Music Hall of Famer's holiday theme song. This holiday number would also remain standard hit fodder for country radio playlists, landing in the top 10 for Tubb again in 1950 and 1951.

With its lonesome message and clever lyrics, "Blue Christmas" spoke more to a country music audience, who embraced heartache, misery, and sorrow. By the midfifties, scores of country music acts were using "Blue Christmas" in their November and December shows. It became the song that put some twang in the mistletoe and garnered the attention of the future King of Rock and Roll.

Before landing at RCA, Elvis Presley had spent a couple of years recording for Sun Records. Sam Phillips, the record label's owner, pitched Presley to both blues and country outlets. Presley's singles were issued with a country side and a blues side. Elvis not only played rockabilly and blues clubs but also toured with country and western acts. Besides hearing Tubb sing "Blue Christmas" numerous times on these tours, the young singer listened to the many others who used the song as a part of their holiday shows. While Elvis loved these country renditions, he sensed that the number couldn't reach its full potential until someone had really put the blues into "Blue Christmas." When he played around with the song in jam sessions, he added a bit of the Memphis beat. In 1957, RCA decided to release an extended-play single with four holiday tunes, and the rocker had a chance to cut "Blue Christmas" his way.

On September 5, 1957, RCA asked Elvis to get into the holiday spirit and cut a quartet of Christmas songs. Even though the producer loved the singer's unique take on "Blue Christmas," it left Presley flat. He was even less excited by the other three cuts, "I'll Be Home for Christmas," "Santa, Bring My Baby Back to Me," and "Santa Claus Is Back in Town." Presley was a perfectionist in the studio and likely believed that the quartet of holiday numbers had not received the effort and time needed to pull off a quality recording. Company executives felt that the results were solid enough to warrant the singer cutting additional holiday songs in order to fill up an entire Christmas album. A few months later, Elvis was shocked to find he had three Christmas hits. Released in November, "Blue Christmas" was a huge hit single—the extended-play 45 topped the EP charts, and the album became RCA's best-selling Christmas album for 1957. "Blue Christmas" drove the sales.

How big was the initial Presley release? According to Jay Johnson's daughter, Judy Olmsted, the rock-and-roll star's recording of Johnson and Hayes' composition generated more royalties in the first year than all the other recordings of "Blue Christmas" had generated up until that point. Scores of other rock, blues, and pop singers raced into the studio to record the song. Thanks to Elvis, the Jay Johnson and Billy Hayes song became the gift that kept on giving to its writers and now keeps on giving to their heirs. Jay Johnson may have missed the mark on many of his songs, yet on a rainy morning in 1947, his vision proved right on target. He understood that Christmas was more than just white; it was also colored by shades of blue.

21

JINGLE BELL ROCK

lmost everyone who listens to "Jingle Bell Rock" agrees that it follows in the tradition of Bill Halley and His Comets' monster single "Rock Around the Clock." The two who were most surprised about this were the song's writers. When Joe Beal and James Boothe penned the number, they didn't have rock and roll in mind at all. The pair of fiftysomething songwriters were shooting for something far more traditional in their lyrics and music — but the surprise was a welcome one!

Boothe was a native Texan educated at USC. A newspaperman with ink in his veins, he covered various news beats while pitching songs to Hollywood producers. Little came of his work until he teamed up with a New Orleans – based broadcasting pioneer whom he met while covering the hot news stories of the day. When these men combined their talents, it would be not as award-winning journalists but as tunesmiths.

Joe Beal was a graduate of Boston University who, after a solid career in newspapers, moved to television. In both forms of media, he was a top-flight reporter. His courageous stand against racial discrimination earned him both praise and scorn.

Sensing a market for Christmas music in motion pictures and television, the men developed several ideas to pitch to Los Angeles producers. All the concepts centered on typical holiday scenes and traditions. The one they kept coming back to was inspired by Currier and Ives paintings and images of newly fallen snow.

With Boothe leading the way, the men imagined what it would be like to take a trip in a sleigh. They sensed that while the snow would cushion their ride, there would also be gentle movement as the sleigh progressed through the streets. This action would cause the passengers to rock from side to side. As everyone thought of jingle bells when riding in a one-horse sleigh, the men combined the rhythmic rocking with the sound of bells. The rest of the imagery, linked lyrically with a nod to the traditional carol "Jingle Bells," fell together.

Beal had a tie with a legendary Nashville producer. The songwriter knew that his friend was working with a new country act that had scored a big crossover hit with "You Are My Special Angel." Beal was also aware that another of the producer's recent discoveries was hot "girl singer" Patsy Cline. The New Orleans scribe shipped the demo to Music City, hoping that the producer might be able to use it with one of his new acts. Beal would quickly discover that his investment in postage would have a big payoff.

Producer Owen Bradley liked what he heard, and felt "Jingle Bell Rock" was a perfect holiday vehicle for Bobby Helms. With country sales sinking — in large part because of Elvis Presley and acts like him taking a new generation of country music fans to rock and roll — the producer saw this song as a way to bridge the gap between the two genres. Helms, however, wasn't so sure he wanted to cut the holiday tune, and he had specific reasons for shying away from the Beal/Boothe song. While Bradley was looking at the short term, Helms was looking at living a dream that began in his youth.

A native of Bloomington, Indiana, Helms began singing with his family act. Hitting local fairs and stage shows, the brothers became local favorites, but their novelty faded as they aged. In 1956, going it alone and deeply entrenched in the country music sound, Bobby Helms made his way to Nashville. He wanted to be the next Ernest Tubb or Hank Thompson and had no ambition to follow other singers who were trying to imitate Presley. As luck would have it, the Hoosier ran into the man who had the power to help him with his dream — Owen Bradley. Bradley, one of the most powerful star markers in Music City, saw Helms' potential and landed the twenty-three-year-old a deal with Decca Records.

Helms topped the charts with a song that appealed especially to soldiers and veterans. "Fraulein" became a number 1 single in country music and, in a move that surprised Bradley and Decca, entered the rock-and-roll charts, topping out at a modest number 36. Even though the chart numbers were much lower on the rock side, the producer and label realized that the much larger rock radio exposure meant "Fraulein" had sold more records to teens than to adults. Because of this demographic, it seemed the rock audience was paying most of the freight. The kids were driving the song's success.

With landing a crossover hit in mind, Decca pitched Helms' "You Are My Special Angel" equally to country and rock-and-roll stations. The song would hit number 1 on the country side and land at number 7 on the rock charts. While the cash-strapped label was thrilled to have a crossover singer, Helms wasn't as sure.

By mid-1957, many country music stations were dropping rock-and-roll records. This was true in the South and West, where country music audiences were the strongest. The clamor for real country music acts was so loud in the industry that it was even creating a divide in Nashville. For a while, anyone with rock-and-roll songs or teenage fans found local clubs and shows off-limits. Even Elvis, whose early RCA releases had topped both country and rock charts at the same time, was banned by some country disc jockeys. This skewing of the market concerned Helms much more than it did producer Bradley.

Helms sensed that his voice and style had a great deal more in common with Eddy Arnold and Hank Williams than with Elvis Presley and Jerry Lee Lewis. He felt he could have a much longer career sticking to a traditional rural sound.

He also believed he was not charismatic enough to be a teen idol and charm audiences on *American Bandstand*. He was concerned that singing a song with "rock" in the title would cause country disc jockeys and fans to turn on him.

Helms let his objections be heard, but it didn't do him much good. Decca needed a hit worse than the company needed to appease a new artist, so Bradley pushed forward with a session to cut the song about a winter's sleigh ride. Working in a small studio on Music Row, with Bradley at piano, the famous Anita Kerr Singers offering vocal backup, and Music City legend Hank Garland on guitar, Helms recorded "Jingle Bell Rock." The singer listened to the demo a couple of times, took the lyric sheet, and with just two microphones, one for Helms and the other for Kerr's group, tackled the new number. Though he was still unsure about the song being right for him, Helms gave the recording all he had. His sincere vocals and rockabilly style produced a tight, easygoing final number.

Helms wondered where "Jingle Bell Rock" would take his career. Bradley left wondering whether he had produced a hit for his struggling employer. "Jingle Bell Rock" shipped in November and jumped onto rock playlists. Teens made the song part of the lineup for their winter dances. In just six weeks, the Helms recording surged into the top 10, landing at number 6 and becoming the dance hit of the season.

Today, "Jingle Bell Rock" is often hailed as the first rock-and-roll Christmas classic. Not only is it the first holiday song to contain the word *rock* in its lyrics, but also the tune made its chart debut at the same time Elvis Presley was lighting up the airwaves with the rocker "Blue Christmas." Elvis's hit was released as an extended-play 45-rpm recording, meaning that the record contained four songs, while Bobby Helms' "Jingle Bell Rock" was shipped as a traditional single. In one respect, Helms' cut would seem to be the winner, since it was a best-selling single. But the fact that Presley's song was played first by most stations and topped the EP charts would seem to give Elvis the edge. If the origins and inspirations of the songs are brought into play, neither might qualify as a true rock-and-roll classic. "Blue Christmas" had big band and pop music as its roots, and when Elvis first heard it, the song possessed a country twang. "Jingle Bell Rock" was also something much different than it seemed. In fact, the rocking had nothing to do with dance steps. Perhaps 1960's "Rockin' Around the Christmas Tree" (recorded in 1958) should claim the honor of being the first real Christmas rock-and-roll record. That is a matter for debate; what can't be debated is the staying power of "Jingle Bell Rock" on the pop and rock charts. In the genre that Helms dearly loved, however, the reaction was much different in 1957.

The reception in country music was not as strong. Many stations, thinking the song was meant only for rock-and-roll dancing, stayed away. Helms' single rolled onto the country best-seller list at number 13, an unlucky number for the young Hoosier. The following week, stations dropped the single, and the song fell from the charts like a lead balloon.

As their song became the most loved rock-and-roll Christmas dance classic of all time, Joe Beal and James Boothe scratched their heads and explained they had never intended "Jingle Bell Rock" to be considered a rocker. The song was about a romantic sleigh ride. As the royalties poured in, however, the songwriters found that this mistake in identity and theme contributed to its success. Since 1957, hundreds of acts have cut the song, and "Jingle Bell Rock" has sold tens of millions of copies. The Christmas rocker was Beal and Boothe's only major hit record, but if they were going to have only one, this was the one to have.

While "Jingle Bell Rock" charted for many more years, no other Helms' record managed to land in the top 40. The Christmas hit had labeled him a rocker, but his voice and style didn't fit the genre at all. Were his fears about cutting the song realized? Was it "Jingle Bell Rock" that stopped Helms' career, or was it his time to fade away? The answer will never be known.

Though never a huge star, until his death in 1997 Bobby Helms continued to perform. His two big hits, "Fraulein" and "You Are My Special Angel," nearly always earned him standing ovations. Yet no matter the time of year, "Jingle Bell Rock" was the song fans most wanted to hear. Helms usually ended his shows with the song that accidentally married rock and roll to Christmas.

22

THE LITTLE DRUMMER BOY

*I*n the more than six decades since it hit the charts, "The Little Drummer Boy" has been adapted and arranged in myriad ways and has become the favorite Christmas standard for millions. It is a musical treat that sparks wonder and thought, and it captures the essence of a gift wrapped in true love.

Gifts are an important part of the holidays, yet few Christmas songs describe having to find the right gift for a special person. Just before World War II, a music teacher was thinking about gifts and how hard it was for people to buy them during the Great Depression. As she contemplated the simple, handmade gifts that poor families placed under the tree, she was inspired to write a song. Although recorded by a family that would inspire one of the most popular motion pictures of all time, the record went nowhere in the 1940s. It would remain undiscovered for two more decades.

Katherine Davis was born in 1892 in St. Joseph, Missouri. She learned piano as a child and wrote songs while still in grade school. She composed her first serious piece of music, "Shadow March," at fifteen. The acclaim she received from that work convinced her to pursue music as a career. At a time when few women graduated from high school, she rode a train more than a thousand miles and enrolled at Wellesley College in Massachusetts. Her creativity and drive impressed her professors. Upon graduation, she was asked to stay at the prestigious school as a music teacher.

Davis had a deep thirst for knowledge and an innate curiosity about history. Her studies expanded the way she looked at life and heavily influenced her compositions. A person could listen to the pacing of one of her melodies and hear the rhythms of the countries and regions she had researched. One month she might be creating something with a classical German feel, and the next month her work might reflect Eastern European folk dances. Sometimes penning as many as two or three songs a week, she was never defined by one particular style.

When World War II broke out in Europe, Davis was deeply troubled. News reports gave detailed accounts of the destruction of many places she had visited on her overseas tours. Trying to push away the horrors of war, she delved into a study of French and English folktales. These tales reminded her of the vibrant and joyous lives of rural villages; times there were simple and quaint in the areas outside of London and Paris until Hitler rained his destruction down from the skies. She longed for the old, simple times again.

One of the stories Davis read taught that no matter how poor one was, someone was always poorer. The moral of the story was that a gift of love from a poor person was worth much more than a bag of gold given by one who was wealthy. Davis realized the lesson firsthand. Many times a child from a poor family had presented her with a simple hug of thanks. That gift had touched the teacher much more deeply than the finest scarf presented by the child of a wealthy family.

The European folktales caused Davis to think back to America's recent Depression. In a world where tens of millions couldn't even afford to buy a Christmas card, a homemade toy made a lasting impact. As she grew older and witnessed such great suffering, she became more convinced that the simple gifts presented by people who had nothing material to give were the most beautiful gifts of all.

With these thoughts in mind, Davis, who often penned complex and intricate musical pieces, sat down at the piano and wrote a simple song about an incredibly humble Christmas gift. Imagining a poor child coming to visit Jesus as he lay in the manger, she penned a poem she called "The Carol of the Drum."

The small boy who was the center of Davis's Christmas song was an insightful child whose only possession was a small drum. He wanted to give an important gift to the new King, but he had nothing — until he played his drum.

The only artists who embraced the song were the Trapp Family Singers. This Austrian vocal group had just escaped Nazi-occupied lands. Because they had lost everything, they fully understood the power of Davis's work. But the von Trapps would not become a viable musical force until

The Sound of Music told their story to the nation. Their RCA release of "The Carol of the Drum" went largely unnoticed.

In 1958, a man who had made his mark arranging music for some of the country's most famous orchestras and big bands formed a new choral group. Harry Simeone was looking for unknown choral pieces to use for an upcoming Christmas album he was recording for Twentieth Century Fox Records. Sensing that voices could blend to create the drumbeat Davis had produced with a piano arrangement, Simeone sat down to rearrange the almost two-decade-old song. The changes he made were so dramatic that he called Davis, and with her approval of his work, the choral director changed the song's name to "The Little Drummer Boy." Simeone's name was added as a cowriter of the new work.

Fox released "The Little Drummer Boy" in November. The choral anthem was placed into a musical stream that included singles such as Ricky Nelson's "Poor Little Fool," Elvis Presley's "Hard Headed Woman," and the Coasters' "Yakety Yak." The Christmas offering about a boy and his drum didn't seem to fit. Yet in the unique world of rock and roll, "The Little Drummer Boy" beat out a spot and became a Christmas hit. Over the next four Christmases, it would climb into the top 40 four more times.

By 1962, the song that had been all but dismissed originally had been recorded by more than a hundred different artists, featured in countless television shows, and adapted into an animated movie starring Greer Garson. Bing Crosby, who passed on the carol when it was first written, made

"The Little Drummer Boy" the last Christmas song he ever recorded.

No one was more shocked by the public's response to "The Carol of the Drum" than Katherine Davis. At the age of seventy, after working for more than five decades in relative obscurity, she was suddenly in the nation's spotlight. Davis died in 1980 and left all the royalties from her compositions, including "The Little Drummer Boy," to the music program at her beloved Wellesley's College of Music. The royalties from "The Little Drummer Boy" have now financed scores of scholarships for students who otherwise could not have studied at the private school.

23

THE CHIPMUNK SONG

*I*n an ironic Christmas twist, the cute and eternally popular "Chipmunk Song" owes its life to an imaginary witch doctor. This African physician and a stubborn real-life rodent paved the way for the creation of a song that has surpassed its association with the holiday to become a year-round franchising machine.

Alvin and the Chipmunks are as well known and beloved as any comic creation of the past fifty years. They have sold more records than many of the acts that reside in the Rock and Roll Hall of Fame. Thanks to Ross Bagdasarian, an American Christmas is not complete without a visit from a trio of talking, dancing, and singing Chipmunks.

Born in Fresno, California, in 1919, Bagdasarian was a fun-loving kid who never lost his childlike view of life. His unique way of seeing the world created a career that continues to bring smiles to children of all ages four decades after his death. His was anything but an overnight-success story. He landed a few small roles on Broadway, but none paid the bills. After cowriting one of Rosemary Clooney's big hits, "Come on-a My House," he failed to score a follow-up hit. He tried acting next. On the big screen, Bagdasarian had minor roles in some really good films, including *Rear Window, The Greatest Show on Earth, Stalag 17,* and *Three Violent People,* but he couldn't land parts that provided anything but a few weeks' worth of income. Bagdasarian rarely had enough money to provide for his growing family.

In 1957, he was down to his last two hundred dollars when he spent all but ten of them on a tape recorder that could vary recording speeds. Using his childlike vision, he wrote a song called "Witch Doctor." Employing his regular speaking voice, as well as a speeded-up version of that voice, Bagdasarian created a stage name of David Seville, recorded his strange and wacky view of teenage love, and found himself with a number 1 hit in the summer of 1958.

The good African physician with his chanting music only bought Bagdasarian a brief moment in the spotlight. The songwriter realized that in order to mount a career in music, he was going to have to create something with lasting value. Rather than turn to the logical road to lasting success, which was serious composition, he began to look for another novelty idea. He was still trying to come up with a fresh concept while on a vacation trip to Yosemite National Park.

It has long been said that nature's wonders have given great men great thoughts. Whether this axiom defines what happened to Bagdasarian is open for debate, since one could argue that he was not a great man and the song spawned from this experience was anything but great music. While in Yosemite, Ross discovered a furry bit of inspiration. The songwriter saw a small chipmunk stubbornly refuse to give up its spot on a California highway bridge, forcing Bagdasarian to wait on the rodent. As he observed the character standing on his back legs and using his chattering voice to scare away anyone who approached, the man laughed. Then he realized the small chipmunk had big-star potential.

Returning to Los Angeles, the determined songwriter used the production technique he had developed for "Witch Doctor" to bring a voice to a stubborn chipmunk. As he discovered, this was a marriage made in musical heaven and one that would change the sound of Christmas forever.

Bagdasarian knew from experience that selling a novelty concept to a major recording label was hard. Most novelty records failed to gain radio play. Only through a stroke of luck and the help of some friends had he found a company willing to take a chance on "Witch Doctor." He needed to craft elements into his new song that would allow him to recreate that energy.

Bagdasarian focused on a Christmas theme and painted a word picture of kids pestering their parents for special presents. In this case, the children were singing rodents and the parent was their human caretaker. This required his adding two more chipmunks, thus creating a vocal trio. As rock and roll was filled with successful singing groups, such as the Platters, the Coasters, and the Fleetwoods, this also fit well into marketing his idea to the musical trend of the moment.

Still, he knew the concept of singing chipmunks was an idea too bizarre for most companies to consider. He had to have another element in his song to get a label behind him.

Bagdasarian's best contacts were at Liberty Records. To get his foot in the studio door, he named his Chipmunks after the three most powerful men at Liberty: Simon Waronker, Theodore Keep, and Al Bennett. It was a stroke of genius, a bit of pandering that paid big dividends as the studio opened its doors for the man and his imaginary rodents.

The Christmas number Bagdasarian wrote was cute, but it needed dialogue to lift it from the status of a children's song to the realm of a release that could find a place on popular radio. The back-and-forth bickering between the father and the problem child, played out between the song's writer and a chipmunk named Alvin, gave the number the energy and humor it needed to get disc jockeys to listen to it. The only reason why many stations opted to play "The Chipmunk Song" was the previous success of "Witch Doctor" — the doctor who opened the door for Alvin, Simon, and Theodore.

While those at Liberty were hoping for a Christmas number that would land in the top 20, Bagdasarian saw his new group as a potential franchise. His drawings reflected the personalities of the creatures. With those in hand, the songwriter put together major marketing plans. He foresaw his Chipmunks' images on everything from lunchboxes to comic books. Even before the record was pressed and shipped, he was planning on producing movies and television specials featuring his colorful rodents.

Released before Thanksgiving of 1958, "The Chipmunk Song" raced up the charts. Part of the reason why it became a huge hit was the recording's special effects. A larger part of this monster Christmas record's success was the humorous attempts of David Seville to keep Alvin, the stubborn member of the group (remember the chipmunk who wouldn't move off the bridge for Ross's car) in line. The good-natured but combative back-and-forth between Alvin and Bagdasarian's characterization of Seville got people of all ages talking. Parents, who were constantly being badgered by their children, saw the song as a scene from their own lives.

The single became a much larger hit than the other big Christmas release of that year, "The Little Drummer Boy," landing at the top of the charts on December 22 and staying there for four weeks. During the monthlong reign, the singing Chipmunks became a national phenomenon, and Bagdasarian spent most of that time signing contracts for everything from clothing lines to stuffed animals.

Thanks to "The Chipmunk Song," Bagdasarian won three Grammys. Six months later, the Chipmunks had their own network show on CBS. Essentially, they were the first rock-and-roll group created by a producer and marketed on TV via a sitcom. The next act to follow them would be the Monkees some four years later, and this formula has since been used countless times by Disney and others.

"The Chipmunk Song" was not a one-year wonder; it

landed on the rock-and-roll charts two more times in the sixties and again almost five decades later. The group that Bagdasarian created defined the man with the unique viewpoint and off-the-wall ideas. Professionally, those in entertainment saw the man as the Chipmunks. Bagdasarian all but lost his own identity in his creation, but he didn't care a bit. He loved being the guy with the trio of energetic and fun-loving woodland creatures.

In 1972, three weeks after another busy Chipmunk holiday season, and fourteen years after he created the trio of loveable rodents, Bagdasarian died of a heart attack. He was just fifty-two. A few years later, his son picked up the mantle as the leader of the unique band. Under the guidance of Ross Bagdasarian Jr., a major Hollywood film featuring the Chipmunks became a blockbuster in 2007. Thanks in part to that movie, the original song grew even stronger. During the next three holidays, "The Chipmunk Song" began to rival "Rudoph the Red-Nosed Reindeer" as the most beloved and played Christmas novelty number. With a second movie proving the lasting box office power of the singing rodents, a new line of merchandise being sold in stores across the globe, and "The Chipmunk Song" now rocking the world of iTunes, the empire Bagdasarian dreamed of is still growing.

The Chipmunks, created as a follow-up to a song about a witch doctor, are hanging as stubbornly on to their fame and place in the Christmas holidays as the original chipmunk held on to its spot on that bridge in 1958. Who knew holding your ground could create that kind of legacy? It took a man with a unique view of life to make chipmunks one of the traditional visitors at Christmas.

ROCKIN' AROUND
THE CHRISTMAS TREE

I n 1958, producer Owen Bradley and Decca Records were excited about Christmas. The year before, Bobby Helms had recorded a huge single, "Jingle Bell Rock." Now they had another song that was the perfect follow-up to the new artist's holiday hit.

Noting the success of "Jingle Bell Rock" and sensing the staying power of rock-and-roll music, Johnny Marks, who had penned the holiday classic "Rudolph the Red-Nosed Reindeer," sat down to create a new song specifically written for the growing teen market. Marks was a formula songwriter. He didn't write from personal experiences but rather created from observations about current trends. He could take a simple hook and quickly transform it into a completed piece.

Almost a decade after he created the song about the red-nosed reindeer, Marks felt he needed a fresh approach to the holidays in order to capture seasonal gold. He was on a New England beach in the summer of 1958 when a group of playful teenagers dancing to an Elvis song provided the inspiration for what would become his second-greatest composition.

As Marks watched the kids dancing in the sand, he wondered if he could top the previous year's rock hit by Bobby Helms. Deciding to give it a try, he returned to his office and dashed off a new melody that was similar to "Jingle Bell Rock" but different enough to set it apart. The tune Marks created was light enough to be enjoyed by adults but hip-sounding to kids. When few melodies were bridging a widening generation gap, this song seemed to have that capability. Marks made sure his latest holiday offering mentioned almost every element of a traditional Christmas, from homemade pie to caroling, and wrapped them up with a bow of young love.

Marks mailed the sheet music for "Rockin' around the Christmas Tree" to Owen Bradley. The songwriter fully expected the producer to have Bobby Helms cut it as a follow-up to "Jingle Bell Rock," but Bradley and Decca Records saw no reason to add another holiday record to Helms' musical resume. History told them that "Jingle Bell Rock" would be an annual Christmas hit for years to come. A new release by Helms would likely dilute the first single's sales by providing Helms' fans and disc jockeys with another choice. Bradley thought it was far better to give the song to an artist who really needed a hit.

In 1958, Brenda Lee was hardly the model for a rock-and-roll star. At thirteen, she was cute and had a rich, full voice and dynamite stage presence. Though teens rarely wanted to listen to a junior high kid, Decca Records had been attempting to make the youngster a national sensation.

Lee was born toward the end of World War II in an Atlanta, Georgia, charity hospital. Weighing just over four pounds at birth, Lee never grew beyond four foot nine. Growing up in a home without running water, and sharing a bed with two other siblings, her life was centered around the only affordable outlet for social outings — church. With a voice that sounded more like that of a sultry adult than that of a tiny child, she sang solos in worship services by the age of three. Capitalizing on her talent, the family often made meal money after services by having Lee sing on street corners.

Her father died in a work accident when she was eight. By that time she had moved from street corner warbler into the role of a local radio star. When the family moved to Ohio, she continued to find work in radio. She would have remained largely unknown, however, if a radio producer had not introduced the child to country music legend Red Foley. Foley was blown away by the small girl with the big voice and signed her to star with him on the syndicated television show *The Ozark Jubilee*. Within a month of her first performance on the show, she was a pint-sized phenom. Newspapers profiled the young star, and record company talent scouts checked her out.

Decca made the first offer because the label believed that a preteen blessed with an adult talent could be a huge sensation in country music. They showcased Brenda with a jazzed-up version of a Hank Williams song and sat back expecting a hit. Disc jockeys all but ignored the single. Next, the label tried a Christmas song, releasing it during the 1956 holiday season, but "Christy Christmas" went nowhere. At the age of twelve, Lee finally broke onto the country charts with "One Step at a Time." After one week in the top 40, that effort died as well. There seemed to be no place for a child in country radio.

With the growth of rock and roll, Decca Records and their top producer, Bradley, opted to push their child star in that musical direction. They had little success. They were desperate for a hit when Marks' "Rockin' around the Christmas Tree" demo arrived at the producer's Nashville office.

On October 19, 1958, Bradley scheduled a session for Lee to cut Marks' holiday song, as well as several other tunes. In order to secure musicians who worked day jobs, the session did not begin until midnight, several hours past the thirteen-year-old singer's normal bedtime. When she arrived at 804 16th Avenue South, the child was eager and ready to work.

Bradley had spared no expense on the session. He brought in the best players in the city, including saxophonist Boots Randolph and guitar picker Hank Garland. He also added the Anita Kerr Singers for backup. To set the mood, he decked out the studio with a Christmas tree and decorations. Rather than record the Christmas number first, Lee cut a few pop standards, including her gutsy take of "(Won't You Come Home) Bill Bailey." With dawn approaching, she was shown "Rockin' around the Christmas Tree."

Using a formula common in Nashville at the time, Bradley played the demo record for Lee and the rest of the group. Once they were familiar with "Rockin'," the musicians worked out their lines, Kerr decided on the harmonies, and Lee looked over the lyrics. In less than thirty minutes, the group came back together to play through and coordinate their take on the song. Working out the different creative views and meshing them into a final arrangement was left to Bradley. With just two microphones in place, the producer counted down and the session began. Less than an hour later, "Rockin' around the Christmas Tree" was finished. Lee then cut the B-side of the record, "Papa Noël."

Decca was so sure that the holiday single would become Lee's first major hit that they pitched it aggressively to disc jockeys at both country and rock stations. Lee was not even a minor star on the national stage, so most ignored the new release. Instead, they replayed Elvis's "Blue Christmas" and Helms' "Jingle Bell Rock." During its initial year of release, "Rockin' around the Christmas Tree" sold fewer than five thousand copies worldwide. Decca lost money on the record.

While it was a disappointment to the studio, Johnny Marks was upset that his "can't miss" number had been wasted on an unknown child star. In an effort to save his song, he began pitching the song to other artists and studios. Most turned the song down, either because it sounded like "Jingle Bell Rock" or because it had already been proven a flop. The song was as dead as a four-week-old Christmas tree.

In today's world, Decca and Bradley would have given up on Lee, as the disc jockeys did the holiday single. But the producer continued to believe that the little girl with the big voice could produce hits. He kept bringing her into recording sessions. In early 1960, a song named "Sweet Nothings" proved that Bradley's faith had been well founded. The fifteen-year-old Lee put that release into the top 10. A few months later, she topped the charts with "I'm Sorry." In the fall, she stormed to number 1 with "I Want to Be Wanted." As Decca looked toward the holidays, Lee was the hottest female act in the country.

Bradley made a call to Decca, suggesting they dust off the old recording of "Rockin' around the Christmas Tree" and give it another spin. The label had nothing to lose and decided to try it again. When it was shipped, there was no mention that it was a rerelease of an older recording. They wanted the public to believe that this was a brand-new Lee record.

The positive reaction of disc jockeys to Lee's holiday tune was in large part because of her recent success. She was all over television, and her concert tours were selling out. Another factor was that Bobby Helms had fallen out of the public eye. "Jingle Bell Rock" was no longer being placed in as heavy a rotation as it had been two years before. Stations were looking for a new holiday rocker, and Lee's two-year-old cut fit the bill.

Unlike Helms, whose career essentially was defined by his holiday release, Lee quickly developed into one of the most influential singers in pop music. At eighteen, she became an international star whose fame was so great that the Beatles once opened for her on a wildly success-ful European tour. Selling tens of millions of albums and singles, the diminutive dynamo made a huge mark on pop, rock, country, and even rhythm and blues charts. A mem-ber of the Rock and Roll Hall of Fame, Lee had monster hits that include timeless classics like "Emotions," "Fool Number One," and "Johnny One Time." But it is "Rockin' around the Christmas Tree" that fans remember most from her career. And why not? The Brenda Lee holiday offering is the fourth-best-selling Christmas single of all time.

25

Do You Hear What I Hear?

Noel Regney had a name that reflected Christmas. The dictionary says that the word *noel* means "a joyful shout expressing exhilaration at the birth of Christ." Through much of his life, Noel rarely found happiness. He grew up in France during the Great Depression. When things looked bleak, he sang and the music lifted his spirits. He wrote songs to express his emotions, desires, and fears. While he was beginning his education as a classical composer, World War II broke out. When the Nazis took Paris, Noel was forced into the German army and made to wear the uniform. On a dark night, he put his civilian clothes back on, escaped from the army camp, and began working with a group of men the world would call the Resistance. Behind enemy lines, he fought the Germans, even helping the Allies during D-Day. Though he was proud to have been a part of driving out oppression, he took no joy in the acts he had been forced to do. He found no glory in battle. His passion for peace eventually led him to write a carol of great hope.

Noel left France after the war in search of a place to further his songwriting career. He found little acceptance and a great deal of rejection. His wanderings finally led him to New York City in the late 1950s. Unable to speak English and without any contacts in America, he stepped into the Beverly Hotel hoping to find a place to stay. By opening that hotel's large main door, he found so much more.

Gloria Shane was playing piano in the hotel dining room that evening. Noel was drawn to the beautiful woman's renditions of popular music. When Gloria took a break, he introduced himself. Though he spoke no English and she spoke no French, they found a common language in the world of music. Within a month they had married.

As they learned each other's language, they discovered there was one goal they shared and one that moved them in different directions. Noel wanted to write classical music, while Gloria had her sights set on becoming a rock-and-roll tunesmith. Within two years, their different viewpoints combined on a Christmas song that not only resonated with people of all ages but also had a classical feel coupled with a modern message.

"Do You Hear What I Hear?" was born because of a nightmare. Noel had believed that the horrors and destruction during the Second World War would wake folks up to the futility of war. Then the Korean War began. When the peace accords dividing North and South Korea were signed, the Frenchman hoped that humankind had finally wised up and that peace would reign on earth. By 1962, Vietnam was in the headlines, and men were dying in a war again.

War scenes depicted on the nightly news caused Noel to spiral into periods of depression. Since the end of World War II, he had been haunted by flashbacks of his time on the battlefield. There was no escape. His nights were filled with the horrors he had witnessed during his time as a resistance fighter. Again and again he saw battles, heard bombs explode, and watched friends die.

Unable to sleep, Noel got up one night and tried to focus on something other than the awfulness of war. Picking up a pen, he tried to write a poem about love. Thoughts of lovers being divided by battles brought the nightmares back to life. He found he couldn't pen anything humorous either. He turned his thoughts to the first Christmas. An idyllic peace flooded his heart as he considered the nativity. Through a story of a child's birth, he was able to escape the nightmares that had been ruling his life for more than twenty years.

Picking up his pen again, Noel wrote a poem that centered on hearing, seeing, and feeling peace. He focused on the birth of Christ as a moment in time when humans experienced a night filled with hope and wonder. After running over his lyrics several times, touching up lines and editing rough phrasing, he showed his Christmas poem of peace to his wife the next morning. As she read it, he asked a favor. He wanted her to write the music.

"Noel said he wanted me to do it because he didn't want the song to be too classical," Gloria told me in a 2001 interview. "I read over the lyrics, then went shopping. I was going to Bloomingdale's when I thought of the first music line."

Over the next few hours, an entire tune was constructed inside Gloria's mind. By the time she got home, her arms filled with the items she had purchased, she believed she had perfectly matched her husband's lyrics with a new melody. She made one mistake, however: she inserted an extra note in each line of the composition. The music didn't fit Noel's lyrics. Noel was so moved by the haunting melody, he decided to rework the lyrics. "Said the wind to the little lamb" became "Said the night wind to the little lamb." The addition added to the song's depth and power.

It was unlike Noel to work with others when composing or reworking his finished compositions. Since he seemed to be in a flexible mood, Gloria pointed out another problem she saw with his lyrics. "I told him that no one in this country would understand 'tail as big as a kite,'" Gloria explained. "Yet he wouldn't change that. As it turned out, he was right. It is a line that people dearly love."

The couple pitched the song to Regent Publishing, owned and managed by the Goodman brothers. Ironically, a man named Noel and a woman named Gloria were pitching a Christmas song to two Jewish men who didn't celebrate the birth of Christ. The Goodmans' brother, Benny, had ridden "Jingle Bells" up the charts almost three decades earlier, so they understood the possibilities of holiday songs. With the Frenchman singing and the American woman playing the piano, the Goodmans listened. What they heard impressed them.

In fact, "Do You Hear What I Hear?" met a specific need.

Harry Simeone, who four years earlier had created the Harry Simeone Chorale and scored a huge holiday hit with "The Little Drummer Boy," was looking for a new Christmas song. The Goodmans called him. Because of their enthusiasm, Simeone asked Noel and Gloria to come directly to his office to play their song for him. This created a dilemma. Gloria had to go to a recording session, and Noel could not play a piano and sing at the same time.

With Simeone looking on, a nervous Noel started and restarted the song several times. When he finally got going, he messed up the phrasing and misplayed the melody. He read in Simeone's eyes all he needed to know. The composer and choir director was not impressed.

Noel and Gloria were shocked when, a few days later, the Harry Simeone Chorale recorded "Do You Hear What I Hear?" Many others were, like Noel and his wife, looking for a reason to hope for peace. With the Cold War, the constant threat of nuclear attack, and the escalating violence in Vietnam, "Do You Hear What I Hear?" struck a chord. The message was so powerful that newspaper stories told of drivers hearing the song on the radio for the first time and pulling their cars off the road to listen.

While the Harry Simeone Chorale hit the pop charts with their cut of Noel and Gloria's song, it took the dean of Christmas music, Bing Crosby, to make the number a real hit in 1963. Thanks to Crosby introducing the song on television, it was arranged for church choirs, became an integral part of television specials, inspired numerous feature articles in magazines, and was even woven into Christmas speeches and sermons.

"We couldn't believe it," Gloria admitted. "So many people wrote us to tell how much the song meant to them. We didn't know that it would cause that kind of outpouring of emotion."

Four decades after they first sang "Do You Hear What I Hear?" for their publisher, Noel and Gloria's song of peace has been recorded thousands of times. "When Robert Goulet came to the line 'Pray for peace, people everywhere,'" Gloria explained, "he almost shouted those words out. It was so powerful!"

The message that Goulet boldly proclaimed was the one Noel wanted the world to understand. The Frenchman didn't want people to just beg for peace; he wanted them to rise up in full voice and demand it. He was sure that was the only way the nightmare of war could be ended.

Noel and Gloria, two songwriters with names so aligned with Christmas, came together to provide the world with one of the great holiday standards. Born of a nightmare, "Do You Hear What I Hear?" is loved because it embraces the dream of peace on earth.

26

PRETTY PAPER

The man whose birth we celebrate at Christmas once told his followers, in Mark 14:7, "The poor you will always have with you." A great many things have changed since Jesus walked the earth, but from generation to generation, those whom he called "the least of these" in Matthew 25:31 – 46 have remained constant in their need. Of the thousands of holiday standards played each year, only a scant few address this issue. One that stands out for its brilliance and stark theme is "Pretty Paper." To fully understand this carol, one must know the background of the musical legend who penned it.

In the late 1950s, Willie Nelson knew what it was like to be poor, having spent most of his life that way. Born during the Depression in the tiny town of Abbott, Texas, Nelson worked odd jobs as a teen, picking up cash wherever he could in an attempt to scratch his way out of poverty. Life grew tougher as he edged into adulthood.

Nelson's grandparents had given the boy a guitar when he was in grade school, and he saw the instrument as a ticket out of a dead-end life. Forming a band, he kicked around dance halls and small-town clubs in Texas and in the state of Washington. During this time, he also peddled clever compositions that revealed his take on everything from love to faith, but his economic situation only grew worse.

Roger Miller once described the life that unknown songwriters lived during those bleak days of the 1950s. Miller spoke of eating catsup sandwiches on good days and living on coffee on the bad ones. Things often grew so desperate for Nelson that he sold his compositions for as little as fifty dollars. Two of these songs, "Family Bible" and "Born to Lose," became monster country music hits, earning millions of dollars in royalties. Nelson received none of the rewards of his work. He remained hungry, poor, and unknown. In 1960, determined to give his music career one more shot, Nelson moved to the Music City.

Nashville was the center of the music industry, and some of the best-known song scribes in the world called it home. Everywhere he turned, other talented souls were armed with scores of tunes, knocking on doors that usually remained locked. Trying to find a place to pitch his original music was even tougher than it had been in Houston. The small, thin, clean-cut man survived only because of the kindness of a few new friends who made sure he had a place to stay and something to eat. The compassion and encouragement he received from these supporters kept him going when he was literally homeless.

A country music legend, Faron Young, was the first to

take one of the compositions Nelson still owned the rights to up the charts. Young's cut of the Texan's "Hello Walls" got Nelson fully on his financial feet. When Patsy Cline recorded Nelson's "Crazy," the songwriter finally realized that almost thirty years of poverty was now visible only in the rearview mirror.

Many in Nelson's situation, now armed with success, would have forgotten about the past and ignored those who were still walking in a poor man's shoes. Yet the redheaded Texan sought out those in need and shared what he had with them. When he saw a homeless man or woman, he saw himself in their eyes. Nelson gave away his time and money to scores of organizations, the most notable being Farm Aid. His efforts to get others involved in reaching out to the needy didn't stop with giving concerts or writing checks. He also took the time to pen a secular Christmas carol that, in a single verse, contained all the sharp social commentary of a Dickens novel.

"Pretty Paper" was unlike any other Christmas song ever written. The chorus described a person caught up in the wonderful activities of the season. The images of wrapping paper, gifts, and heartfelt expressions of love punctuated a story that spoke of the normal holiday activities, but an underlying second theme — almost hidden in the verse — pointed to a Christmas that was much different.

In just a few subtle lines, Nelson presented a man, either unnoticed or ignored by shoppers, sitting on the streets. He is a lost soul riddled with pain, hunger, and hopelessness.

He prays that someone during the celebration of Christ's birth will notice him and provide him with the simple gift of compassion. One person sees the homeless man, but rather than stop, they rush by, focused on their own agenda. The poor man is left crying on the streets.

Nelson almost disguised his intent too well. As he pitched the song, most who heard "Pretty Paper" were so caught up in the message of a person wrapping gifts for loved ones, they missed the comments about reaching out to those who had nothing at Christmas. The song's haunting line "Should I stop, better not, much too busy" was completely lost on them. Others who recognized the song's real message were made uncomfortable by the thought of those in need. Bringing this carol to the public's attention took another Texan who had experienced years of tough living.

Roy Orbison spent more than a decade trying to establish his career as a rock-and-roll singer. Scores of hopeful steps had led to mostly locked doors in Texas and Memphis. By 1963, with hits such as "Only the Lonely," "Running Scared," "Crying," and "Dream Baby," the man with the dark sunglasses from Wink, Texas, had arrived. His popularity had grown to the point where he was a huge star, not just in America but also in Europe and Japan. Even the Beatles came to watch him perform when he landed in Britain.

Orbison was one of the most unique talents in music. He was not a traditional rocker or a great showman. What he possessed was a voice laced with emotion that soared to heights few male vocalists could hit. He was one of rock music's few tear-jerk artists whose songs often reflected the pain and disappointment of failed love. He was a perfect fit for Nelson's Christmas story of a forgotten man.

In 1963 — a decade before Nelson would become a famous singer in his own right — Orbison cut "Pretty Paper" and shipped it to radio stations in time for the holidays. The recording's chorus was so well constructed and produced that those who heard it were captured by the song's message of buying and wrapping a gift for a loved one. The image was so strong that most missed the verse's story of the lost, needy soul whose plight was being ignored during the holidays. Like the man Nelson had written about, the message of "Pretty Paper" was almost completely lost in the holiday's busy shuffle.

Orbison's holiday release quickly jumped onto the charts and made it to number 15 on the rock-and-roll best-seller list. It was also picked up by a large number of pop music and country music outlets. This song continues to be an important part of the holiday music rotation at pop and country radio stations. Few realized that "Pretty Paper" was not just another musical tale about holiday love. This inaccurate view of the secular carol would not begin to change until the escalation of the homeless problem was recognized by the news media in the early 1980s. Finally, Nelson's subtle message wrapped into a beautifully crafted package began to make the impact the songwriter intended.

"Pretty Paper" is brilliant in its simplicity, and its theme encapsulates all that is right and wrong with the modern holiday season. The song reflects the love that is a part of Christmas, while shining a spotlight on the ones who are forgotten during this time. In a sense, it is a musical version of a Frank Capra movie, without the happy ending. The man on the street has no angel looking out for him. In "Pretty Paper," the wonderful life is reserved for some, while others are caught in a cold, unforgiving world without the joy of Christmas.

Willie Nelson knew both sides of this equation, and his eyes saw those whom others didn't notice. In "Pretty Paper," he created a vehicle to open the eyes of millions to this situation, and a few of them, inspired by the message, at last chose to stop and make an impact!

Let There Be
Peace on Earth

hristmas is filled with songs that were not written for the holidays. "Sleigh Ride," "Let It Snow," "Frosty the Snowman," "These Are a Few of My Favorite Things," and "Winter Wonderland" are just a few of the seasonal favorites that never mention Christmas. While fun and entertaining, most of these numbers are weightless in their message, meant to be nothing more than an entertaining glance at a situation or event connected to winter. However, one song associated with Christmas was written for a much deeper purpose. The lyrics contain not only a hope for peace but also a formula for getting there. This incredible hit was born out of a deep, dark period of despair.

Christmas is often not a day of joy. Suicide rates are higher during the holidays than at any other time of the year. Many struggle with loneliness and depression. Even as people say, "Peace on earth," internally they are waging a war to find peace of heart and mind.

In the days just before the conclusion of World War II, Jill Jackson was struggling. Her husband had left her. She was broke. A single mother drowning in sorrow and pain, Jill felt she was on a battlefield with no hope of escaping. Christmas had never seemed so dark. Words of cheer did nothing to ease her depression. She wondered, why bother to live at all?

Life had never been easy for the young woman. Her mother died when she was three. When her father remarried, he and his new wife decided they didn't want a child weighing them down. They took her to the local authorities and gave the little girl away. Before she went to school, Jill could read the writing on the wall — she was unworthy of love. Being a ward of the state constantly reinforced this belief.

Jill prayed for a family to rescue her, yet when other children were adopted, she was passed over. She learned to mask her disappointments. She pretended to be a young girl who didn't need anyone else. When she was finally on her own, she traveled to Hollywood and found work in motion pictures. She found roles in western movies and married a film director. When her daughter was born, Jill felt she was living a fairy tale. She had an incredible home and was part of a social circle that included many of the biggest stars in Hollywood. She seemed to be wanted and loved by everyone.

She would soon discover that her happiness was a fleeting illusion. Jill's husband left her for another woman.

Feelings of abandonment rushed back into her life. She was once again the little girl no one wanted.

Unable to cope with all the disappointments in her life, Jill tried to commit suicide. She nearly succeeded but was revived. Sadly, she was also partially paralyzed.

The peace she had sought through death morphed into even more pain. Jill was not only unwanted; she was a cripple. The dark thoughts whispering inside her head grew even louder. The need for a release from this mental war grew even greater.

She was once again on the brink of suicide when she began to read the words of Jesus. In the Bible, she found an acceptance she had never known on earth. Thanks to her newborn faith, she began to see herself as a person of value. As peace came into her life, her self-inflicted injuries began to heal as well. For the first time, she took off the mask of pretending she was someone she wasn't and let the world see the beauty even her own father had missed.

One of those who noticed the beauty of the woman was Seymour "Sy" Miller. The Brooklyn-born Miller was a music arranger and producer for Warner Brothers. Best remembered for writing TV theme songs and preparing night club acts for Debbie Reynolds, Andy Williams, Danny Kaye, and Joel Gray, Sy was an all-around musical genius. But it was Miller's character, more than his talent, that made the greatest impact on Jill.

After Jill and Sy married, she too began to dabble in music. Rather than attempt to create popular songs, as her husband did, she opted to write for children. A generation before Fred Rogers opened the door of television to good neighbors, Jill composed songs that trumpeted the value of each person's life. These educational messages of peace and understanding were published in school music books and recorded on Little Golden Records. For the first time, Jill was making a positive impact. Life was worth living.

The forties became the fifties, and war broke out again, this time in Korea. Though Jill was now at peace with herself, her heart broke as she watched women lose their husbands in battle and children face life without fathers. It seemed the world was still as bent on destroying itself as she had been when she tried to take her own life. If she could find peace in her own tormented life, then why couldn't the world's leaders?

Finding herself again sinking into depression, she once more turned to songwriting in an effort to find some peace. On a break from her work, she read that a group of teenagers from all over the world would soon be attending a brother-hood camp not far from her California home. She realized that getting people to come together in acceptance was the way to stop war. With this thought in mind, she roughed out a song she called "Let There Be Peace on Earth." Her husband added a choral arrangement.

Thanks to her success in children's publishing, the organizers of the brotherhood camp welcomed a visit from her to their facilities. Jill impressed the gathering with her anthem of peace. When she offered to teach it to the campers, she was given the green light. A few weeks later, on a beautiful summer evening, a group of 180 teenagers of all races and religions formed a circle and sang this new song for the first time. A few newspapers released stories on the camp and mentioned the program that included "Let There Be Peace on Earth." Jill thought the publicity would open the door to others singing her song and adopting its message. But it didn't happen. After that initial performance, the song all but died.

For years, Jill and Sy tried to give the song away to school and church choirs. No one would take it. As a new generation of men began dying in Vietnam, people finally discovered "Let There Be Peace on Earth." Reading the words, choir directors realized the power of Jill's thoughts. Peace did begin with each individual. This was a life lesson that churches and youth leaders wanted to share with kids. If they could get that thought ingrained in the minds of young people, then other generations would follow the kids.

The song began to spread through church and high school choirs around the country. The United Auto Workers, the American Legion, B'nai B'rith, the Kiwanis Clubs, and CORE began to sing it at their meetings. Five years later, the song had been translated into scores of languages and had become popular in Holland, England, Italy, France, Germany, Lebanon, Japan, India, and several nations in Latin America.

With choirs singing it, entertainers soon took the song

into the recording studios. Ernie Ford, Andy Williams, Danny Kaye, Nat King Cole, the Smothers Brothers, Roy Rogers, Dale Evans, Eddie Albert, Edie Adams, Gladys Knight, Mahalia Jackson, Bob Hope, and more than a hundred other artists cut it. With so many different versions being played on radio at the same time, no single ever became a huge hit. But when taken together, the combined sales of "Let There Be Peace on Earth" made it one of the best-selling songs of the era. Even more impressive was its incredible sheet music sales.

After the end of the Vietnam War, "Let There Be Peace on Earth" seemed to have run its course. Yet radio disc jockeys couldn't resist pulling Jill Jackson's song out at Christmas. Within a generation, the song of peace was appearing on scores of new Christmas albums. Perhaps the most successful and hauntingly poetic version was the one Vince Gill took up the Christmas charts. To emphasize the power of Jackson's words and the need for the song's message to be carried on to the next generation, he arranged his version as a duet he performed with his daughter.

The reason why "Let There Be Peace on Earth" has been adopted as a holiday favorite is that its message echoes what Christmas is supposed to be about. As Jill Jackson's song clearly explains, if each person on earth vows to initiate peace in their own world, then all wars will end. In "Let There Be Peace on Earth" — a song written by a woman who understood the anguish of not knowing peace and who fought a daily struggle with mental depression — the formula for peace is there. The question the song really asks each year is, who will be the first to adopt its principle as their own, not just at Christmas but on every day of the year?

HOLLY JOLLY CHRISTMAS

fter writing "Rudolph the Red-Nosed Reindeer," Johnny Marks sensed the potentially huge market in creating Christmas songs. With that in mind, he quickly formed the St. Nicholas Music Publishing Company and went to work composing more holiday classics. Beginning in 1952, he found some success with "When Santa Claus Gets Your Letter," "The Night Before Christmas Song," and "The Santa Claus Parade." While Chuck Berry's version of Marks' "Run Rudolph Run" received some moderate airplay, none of Marks' new songs came close to approaching the success of his first about the reindeer. When he scored a holiday chart topper in 1962, with Brenda Lee's "Rockin' around the Christmas Tree," he cemented his status as "Mr. Christmas" in the songwriting world. If Marks, who was Jewish, saw the irony in having earned this label, he never let on. It seemed no one loved the holiday as did Marks.

With "Rudolph" and "Rockin' around the Christmas Tree," Marks could have sat back and enjoyed his success. But the songwriter was bent on creating even more holiday magic. That opportunity came when he was asked to produce the music for a television special centering on the life of Rudolph. In the video version of "Rudolph the Red-Nosed Reindeer," a host of new characters and situations were introduced. This expanded version of the old story gave the imaginative Marks all the fodder he needed to produce a number of lively songs.

The stop-action production technique employed in the thirty-minute special had been a Hollywood staple since the silent era. The most famous motion picture to use the painstaking process was the original *King Kong.* With stop-action, three-dimensional figures were created and then moved one frame at a time on a set. Not only did body positions need to be moved, but also facial expressions and background details needed to be changed to fit the action. The process was difficult and expensive.

Rankin/Bass Productions was in charge of creating the characters and staging the special effects. NBC signed on to air the special. Halfway through production, those underwriting the cost of *Rudolph* grew nervous. They doubted the show's ability to recoup its high production costs and began looking for a way to gain the needed publicity to assure that an audience would tune in for the special.

At the time, most cartoon voices were created by actors primarily known for their work in radio. Casting a popular personality as one of the voices was unheard of, but a sponsor suggested that a celebrity could add credibility to the final product. However, the cast was already set. Without any additional roles to fill, they needed to rewrite the script to include another character who could be voiced by a celebrity. The writers decided to add a snowman narrator. The actor signed to play the part bore a stronger resemblance to Santa than to a snowman.

Burl Ives was born on an Illinois farm in 1909. Though bright and athletic, Ives had a bit of the gypsy in his soul. In 1930, he dropped out of college and began wandering around America. He established a pattern of working a few odd jobs, playing his banjo and singing folk songs at dances, and then thumbing his way to the next town to start all over again.

It took a decade for Ives to settle down. He acted in plays, sang on the radio, and even made a few records. The big man with the powerful voice finally began to get some traction when he headlined a radio show called *The Wayfaring Stranger.* From there, he landed a recording contract and produced a string of folk records. His big break came when he was drafted into military service. As a soldier, he was cast in Irving Berlin's movie *This Is the Army.* Thanks to the contacts he made during the experience, by the late 1940s Ives was making his mark in motion pictures. One of his songs, "Lavender Blue," was nominated for an Academy Award in 1950. The nomination opened doors for him to perform on Broadway. A dynamic presence on screen and stage, he gained worldwide fame as Big Daddy in *Cat on a Hot Tin Roof* and then, a year later, won a supporting actor Oscar for *The Big Country.*

With an impressive resume, Ives was brought in to "save" *Rudolph*. As production had been all but completed, his role was one of the most unusual of his career. He was given a reworked script. His newly created character appeared, by himself or interacting with others, only in very small segments of the film. Since the songs for the program had been arranged and recorded, he also had no say in the music. When he went into the recording studio, he simply listened to what the other actors had recorded, then sang along with music that had the lead vocals "wiped clean." Ives had never been so disconnected from the process of making a film.

One of the songs Ives was asked to rerecord was a number Marks had quickly put together. "Holly Jolly Christmas" was like cotton candy — lacking weight and substance. In the music world, it was known as a formula song. Marks simply took a hook of two rhyming words that had long associations with Christmas, *holly* and *jolly*, and worked out a clever, catchy melody to go with them. The final lyrics didn't center on anything more than a passing glance at the emotions of the season. "Holly Jolly Christmas" seemed little more than filler — and it may have been forgotten if not for Ives.

With more than three decades of experience as a folk singer, Ives had a feel for music. He especially understood pacing and vocal flow. When he combined his skills as an actor with his musical talents, he transformed a song into an adventure in storytelling. To Ives, the simple, upbeat lyrics of "Holly Jolly Christmas" reflected a mixture of the innocent charm of the holidays combined with a bit of the prankish nature of snowball fights and secretly imbibing a bit of holiday cheer. He carefully shaped his vocal inflections to create a character who was living out those thoughts. With his pacing and easygoing style, Ives made the song his own. This accomplishment was remarkable, given that he had no control over the previously recorded music tracks or the arrangement.

After production, Ives promoted the special. His name and his prestige as an Academy Award winner were pushed in the press releases. The ploy elevated *Rudolph*'s status exactly as planned.

When *Rudolph the Red-Nosed Reindeer* aired in December 1964, it garnered a fifty-fifty audience share. In other words, it was a huge hit. Critics noted that while the special was certainly cute, Ives' voice brought Sam the Snowman to life and caught the attention and hearts of audiences. The last-minute ploy of using a celebrity had worked so well that the practice would be employed in almost every animated special that followed.

NBC rescheduled *Rudolph* for the 1965 holidays. With a full year's warning, Ives saw an opportunity to take his few days' work on the special and turn them into a gold mine. Booking time in the studio, he recut "Holly Jolly Christmas" with a new, contemporary arrangement and snappier orchestration. In November, the single shipped to radio stations.

Ives used guest appearances on television programs to plug his new single. This exposure, combined with the second running of *Rudolph the Red-Nosed Reindeer*, made "Holly

Jolly Christmas" the year's biggest holiday hit. But the best was yet to come.

The thirty-minute special featuring the world's most famous reindeer garnered such high ratings in its second showing that the network quickly lined it up for a return the following year. The special became a regular part of Christmas programming every year.

The television special's annual appearances gave Ives and his special holiday song a free yearly publicity boost. With each new holiday season, "Holly Jolly Christmas" gained even more exposure. Thanks to *Rudolph*, the song has been passed from one generation to the next.

What was supposed to be a few days' worth of voiceover acting turned into a lifetime gig for Burl Ives. Today, his 1959 Oscar for *The Big Country* is almost forgotten, and his "A Little Bitty Tear" is rarely played on even oldie radio stations. Few remember him from his television and movie roles. But most people recognize the unforgettable contribution he made to "Holly Jolly Christmas."

WE NEED A LITTLE CHRISTMAS

hen people picture the holidays, they often imagine a scene created by Currier and Ives, the famed American artists of the 1800s. Their pastoral winter images usually embrace snow, trees, sleighs, and rural locations. People also envision scenes from classic Hollywood films, such as *It's a Wonderful Life*, *Holiday Inn*, or *Christmas in Connecticut*, whose sets transport folks from the bustle of the big city and into a quieter town.

Still, New York City dresses up for the holidays and embraces the spirit of the season like few other places on the planet. Just before Thanksgiving, the Big Apple is transformed into a brightly decorated shopper's paradise and a winter wonderland of joy. The streets, which are often so impersonal, become alive with smiles and voices singing out holiday greetings to complete strangers.

Easily passed from one person to another, the Christmas spirit is infectious. It's found in shop windows, in Central Park sleigh rides, on the tongues of street musicians, and in the thousands of street corner Santas ringing their bells and crying out, "Merry Christmas!" From the Rockettes' lively holiday dance lines to the churches' resounding bells, Christmas fills the streets around the island of Manhattan.

For four years, beginning in May 1966, a Christmas song was sung every day on Broadway. This little number was so contagious that theater patrons, even days after seeing the show and wiping their brows in the midst of summer heat, could not get the tune out of their heads. And it seemed that every person who hummed it had to smile. Though Angela Lansbury introduced Broadway's most famous carol when LBJ was in the White House, the roots of its inspiration go back to the days of FDR.

In 1931, in the midst of the Great Depression, Jerry Herman was born in New York City. With a quarter of the American workforce unemployed, soup lines in every major city, and migrant workers constantly moving while looking for their next job, times were tough. In this era of insecurity, depression was not only an economic reality but also a state of mind. Millions had given up hope.

Herman was born into a family that had the money to provide a nice home, good food, and new clothes. Herman was taken to Broadway shows when he could barely walk. The older he grew, the more he realized that while he lived in a world filled with dreams, many kids lived in a world of nightmares.

The United States was in the midst of World War II when, as a teen at the Stissing Lake Camp in the Berkshire Mountains, Herman directed the amateur productions. He thrived on the team approach they needed. Because many kids had fathers and brothers fighting in the war, these productions were vehicles of escape. The music and laughter had the same effect as a holiday present being unwrapped. For a few minutes, the world was filled with wonder and joy. Even at this young age, Herman understood that a healthy escape was a gift everyone needed from time to time.

Herman wrote music in high school and continued to compose songs throughout his days as a student at the University of Miami. Graduating from college at twenty-one, he returned to New York. Within months, Herman's *I Feel Wonderful* opened in Greenwich Village. Beginning on October 18, 1954, the musical ran for forty-eight performances. While *Wonderful* wasn't a great success, the show opened doors of opportunity for the young man whom critics and producers were calling the Boy Wonder.

Within seven years, Herman had a legitimate Broadway hit with *Milk and Honey*. It was his third show, *Hello, Dolly!* that made him the toast of the Great White Way. The original production, starring Carol Channing, ran for 2,844 performances from January 16, 1964, to December 27, 1970.

Even as *Hello, Dolly!* was drawing in crowds, Herman introduced a new musical. His *Mame* was based on a play by Jerome Lawrence and Robert E. Lee. Before that, *Mame* had been a successful novel by Patrick Dennis. The book, play, and musical all centered on the tale of an eccentric woman who lived in luxury on New York City's Upper East Side until the Great Depression wiped her out. Within the dark themes running through the book and play, Herman sensed a chance to create a bright comedy filled with unique characters.

When writing *Mame*, Herman realized that the scenes after the fall of the stock market needed to lift people. But how does one crawl out of a Depression? What brings true happiness? Herman realized that the play needed a big dose of "the most wonderful time of the year."

As he was growing up in New York City, the writer had noted that Christmas was able to transform lives and moods even in the midst of the uncertainty of the Depression and World War II. He had seen the bright looks on poor children's faces when charity organizations handed them even the simplest of gifts. To those kids, it didn't matter that it was December 17 rather than December 25. They had experienced Christmas. As Herman wrote in his autobiography, "You don't have to wait for a special day to celebrate Christmas. It was more important to celebrate Christmas when you need it." Certainly, as he wrote the play, Herman saw a world that needed to smile, laugh, and know joy again.

The mid and late 1960s were a time of upheaval in the United States. The Vietnam War, the integration of schools, the assassinations of prominent politicians and social leaders, and the threat of another world war — this time with the Soviet Union — had everyone on pins and needles. Many television preachers were warning people that these were "the end times." Millions were depressed, feeling as if the best days of life were behind them. Suicide rates were rising dramatically. And no one seemed able to discover a way to bridge the generation gap. Worst of all, Americans were finding more ways to divide rather than unite.

Even the normally upbeat Herman was pulled down by the images on the TV news and the gloom in the faces on New York streets. And then the Christmas holidays arrived. While the news hadn't grown any brighter, Herman noted that during the season, the mood had. The mere mention of Christmas brought hope to those who were sure the world was ending.

Herman was a perfectionist who spent months writing and rewriting his songs. "We Need a Little Christmas" flowed out of him as if it were a tune he had been singing for years. He would later write in his autobiography that the song "brought out inner strengths in that woman [the lead in *Mame*] that she didn't even know she had — that I didn't even know she had." In a sense, the character Herman had created in his musical wrote the song for him. This message of hope was perfect for the musical, but what he didn't know was how it would resonate with everyone who came to Broadway to catch his latest work.

"We Need a Little Christmas" made its appearance about midway through the first performance of *Mame*. The scene involved the cast of characters coming to grips with the stock market crash of 1929. Surrounded by doom and gloom (much like the environment on the streets outside the theater), Mame found reason to hope. She declared that what the world needed was a little Christmas spirit "right this very minute." She believed that this would help bring back the happiness dashed by Wall Street's blackest day. With a smile on her face and a spring in her step, Mame cried out for everyone to "haul out the holly" and "fill up the stocking" and then added a plea for Old St. Nick to make his rounds early, as "Santa, dear, we're in a hurry."

"We Need a Little Christmas" struck a chord that night on Broadway and each time it was heard thereafter. The song lifted spirits all across America. Several versions of it, recorded by Andy Williams, Julius La Rosa, and the New Christy Minstrels, found instant airplay in late November. With its easy-to-remember lyrics, an unforgettable tune, and a message that erased doubts and fears, it was the perfect song for such imperfect times. "We Need a Little Christmas" became an immediate classic and was still charting on popular playlists in 2009.

Herman saw what kept happening in New York during the Depression, World War II, and the sixties and realized that this was mirrored all across the country. Sensing the thirst for inspiration and recognizing the gift of joy and hope brought annually by the holidays, he crafted a song that embraced a message he believed. It's true that we need a little Christmas every year, and Herman's song helps us accomplish that wonderful goal.

30

MERRY CHRISTMAS, DARLING

ometimes it takes a musical carpenter to finish building a song someone else has started. This was truly the case with "Merry Christmas, Darling." For twenty years, it was an uncompleted project—a great concept set to a musical score that simply couldn't carry it up the national playlists. Then a college professor gave a student the challenge of creating a new musical platform for his lyrics. Within five years, the carol of love topped the holiday charts.

It all began in 1946, when two teenagers shared a few innocent moments during a summer vacation in the Midwestern town of Northfield, Minnesota. With the world at peace, dreams had replaced the nightmares of war. Frank Pooler was dreaming of two things. The first was a career in music, and the second was a young woman he had met that summer, named Sylvia.

Sylvia was spending the summer visiting family when she and Pooler met. There was an instant attraction. After three months of movies, long walks, hand-holding, and talking about future dreams, the real world interrupted the budding romance. Sylvia returned to her home in Wisconsin to begin her school term, while Frank spent the last two weeks of summer alone before returning to St. Olaf College.

"I was fishing one day out in a lake," Pooler explained in a 2003 interview, "and though it was nowhere near Christmas, a lyric came to me. Guess I was thinking about what it would be like to spend a holiday separated from someone you loved."

Frank's love poem, which he called "Merry Christmas, Darling," embraced the same sentiment found in the recent wartime holiday hit "I'll Be Home for Christmas." Pooler's version, while simply written, was longer and more detailed than the Bing Crosby hit. The teen's song examined in detail the heartache created by separation. After refining his lyrics, the young man composed a melody and completed a musical arrangement. He then made a mental note to create a second copy to send to his summer love. Yet he wouldn't follow through for more than twenty years. Only after he graduated from St. Olaf would "Merry Christmas, Darling" be remembered again.

"I was working in Boston with a vocal group," Pooler recalled, "and the trio was looking for a Christmas song. I told them I had written one. They heard it, liked it, sang it, and I got 'Merry Christmas, Darling' published."

Never recorded, his holiday love song was heard by few outside of Boston. As the years passed, Pooler married, moved across the country to California, and became a college instructor, and the song was filed away. There it would have remained if Pooler had not been drawn into a conversation with one of his students at California State University, Long Beach.

In Pooler's mind, Richard Carpenter was a genius — a man possessed who was driven to write, arrange, and perform. Carpenter had a refined ear and a quick mind that could listen to a simple melody and transform it into a symphony. He ate, slept, and lived music. Nothing could interrupt his focus. While taking a full course load, Carpenter found the time to put together a small group. His Richard Carpenter Trio performed in local clubs and theaters. The group featured Wes Jacobs and Richard's younger sister, Karen, on drums and vocals.

"One day as the holidays approached," Pooler explained, "Richard told me he was tired of his group doing standards like 'White Christmas.' He wanted to know if I knew of anything different and new his group could sing. I thought for a moment, then told him I had written a Christmas song a long time ago, but I didn't care much for the tune."

The student took Pooler's song into a room so small, it could barely hold a piano and a bench. Locked in that tiny space, he took twenty-year-old lyrics and matched them with a new melody. In the process, he created a stable musical foundation on which to build his professor's timeless message of lost love.

Pooler approved Carpenter's work, encouraging him to use the Christmas song with his trio. With Richard's sister,

Karen, singing, the new version of "Merry Christmas, Darling" was used a half-dozen times in the group's December shows. This was the time when hard rock was beginning to take over many radio playlists and the world had been splintered by Vietnam, race riots, and a generation gap, so it seemed the wrong time for a light jazz combo to make waves in entertainment. The old song with the new melody was laid aside and forgotten again as Carpenter worked on refining his group and landing a record deal.

After a couple of false starts with RCA, the trio, now known simply as the Carpenters, got backing from A&M Records. Recognizing Richard's unique talent and drive, they allowed him a great deal of freedom in choosing and arranging the group's music and orchestrating the recording sessions. A&M's faith in the young man's ability paid off. The Carpenters' first big hit, "Close to You," topped the charts in 1970.

At a time when most rock groups reflected the counterculture, the Carpenters were clean-cut and mainstream. They were closer to the music of Andy Williams than to that of Jimmy Hendrix or Creedence Clearwater Revival. Thanks to Richard's incredible arrangements and Karen's mellow, sincere vocals, the group carved out a niche that made them one of the strongest forces in the entertainment world. Four months after their first single, "We've Only Just Begun" made the group a national sensation.

A&M Records was thrilled with the cross-generational popularity of the Carpenters. Their fans didn't represent a niche audience; they represented every facet of America. While many hard rockers would never have been accepted in the holiday market, the Carpenters' fans were demanding that the group cut a Christmas song. A&M's marketing department also saw the potential of a marriage between the group and the holidays and asked for a seasonal single.

Making the request and having it fulfilled were two different things, however. The Carpenters were so popular, they were playing long strings of one-night stands, living in hotels and staying away from the studio for months at a time. While the idea of a Christmas song was a good one, when it could be produced was a huge problem. Seizing the one open week the group had in their schedule, A&M producer Joe Osborne booked a studio. Not having any new material at his fingertips, Osborne was simply going to ask Richard to rework an old standard with one of his magical arrangements and then cut it in a hurry.

Richard was a perfectionist who often spent weeks creating and refining his work. He didn't like to be pushed. While the fans would likely buy a quick, generic Carpenters' version of "White Christmas" or "Silver Bells," that seemed like a sellout to the young man. Rather than do things the easy way, the group's leader returned to the lyrics Frank Pooler had written more than two decades earlier.

The Carpenters believed that recording "Merry Christmas, Darling" was the only choice, given the time constraints. Richard had already arranged the song, and the group knew it well. The song was a fresh number, one the public had never heard, so it was a Carpenters record and not a rehash of someone else's hit. And with this familiar song, Richard felt he could match the quality of all other Carpenters' projects.

A&M had been hoping for something quick and adequate to satisfy the nation's craving for the Carpenters. Thanks to Richard's work ethic and attention to detail, what they received was a holiday song and performance that exceeded their expectations. "Merry Christmas, Darling" possessed a flowing score with rich layers of harmonies and orchestration. Added to this musical effort were Karen's dynamic vocals. She breathed life into each one of Pooler's lyrics as if she had become the person so desperate to be with the lost love of her life. Thanks to this marriage of talent and effort, "Merry Christmas, Darling" was a holiday love letter — both timely and timeless — and became the most popular Christmas release of the decade.

In 1978, the Carpenters recorded an album, *Christmas Portrait*, that contained a new version of "Merry Christmas, Darling." What came out of those sessions was one of the best recordings of the pop rock era. All of the songs Richard arranged and the group cut struck deep a chord with listeners. Even as stations played Carpenter versions of carols such as "O Little Town of Bethlehem" and "O Holy Night," people continued to request "Merry Christmas, Darling." By the time Karen passed away in 1983, the Carpenters' carol had established itself as a vital musical element of each new holiday season. The Carpenters' stamp is so firmly imprinted on the song that few others have jumped into the studio to record it. Almost four decades after it was first cut, it remains the property of the group.

It took twenty years for a pair of college students from two different generations to come together and create this incredible Christmas classic. It took another five years before Pooler and Carpenter's song first found its holiday niche. But, like Christmas itself, some things are worth the wait.

31

GRANDMA GOT RUN OVER BY A REINDEER

blizzard brought together the forces needed to create Christmas's most bizarre hit song. In the midst of a blinding snowstorm, two men met. One shared a number he'd been singing for some time. The other listened intently, convinced he was hearing a future hit. For the quirky song about a grandmother's tragic accident to gain national exposure, however, there would need to be a series of protests, a huge gamble, a homemade music video, and holiday luck.

Randy Brooks and his band had just finished a one-week booking in Lake Tahoe in 1978. As they loaded up for their next gig, a snowstorm hit the area. The snow closed the roads and stranded the band at their hotel. With nothing but time on his hands, Brooks headed back to the club he had called his musical home for the past week and stumbled on an unknown songwriter.

Several years before being stranded at Lake Tahoe, Brooks had been challenged. He was told that no major hit song had ever begun with a tragic death. Once death was inserted into lyrics, people quit listening. The only exceptions to this rule were songs, such as "El Paso" or "Tell Laura I Love Her," where the death occurred late in the story. Brooks was determined to develop a concept that would go against this long-established songwriting rule. Where to start? What hook would allow him to navigate an area that seemed to offer only failure?

In 1973, country music superstar Merle Haggard had penned an unusual hit called "If We Make It through December," a sincere song about a poor family trying to simply hang on until the end of the year.

With that song in mind, Brooks began work on a new number. He decided that a grandmother's tragic death would be the anchor in the first verse. The manner of her demise would be shocking. The elderly woman became inebriated on eggnog at a family Christmas Eve gathering. While staggering home through the snow to retrieve her medicine, she was struck by a reindeer. Brooks worked into the song a wide variety of holiday traditions, casting each in a humorous light. The end joke would be that while many might not believe in Santa, after seeing the cause of Grandma's death, this family had complete faith that the jolly old elf was real.

Brooks finished the novelty number, which leaned more toward the wacky humor of Ray Stevens than toward the sincere earthiness of Merle Haggard. The song was genuinely funny, but its dark humor hardly seemed the vehicle needed to defy the rules against songs about death selling in the world of music. Brooks taught the lyrics and easy-to-sing melody to his band. While audiences laughed at the premise, record labels weren't interested.

On stage that snowy night in Lake Tahoe was a blue-grass group that leaned toward comedy. Elmo 'n' Patsy's zany blend of music and humor impressed Brooks.

After the final song, Brooks wandered backstage to meet Elmo Shropshire of the band. Over the next hour, the pair exchanged road stories, talked of their musical influences, and even spoke of dreams. Toward the end of the night, Brooks shared his holiday novelty number. Shropshire loved the song. Having Elmo 'n' Patsy — who didn't have a record deal or much of a following — latch onto the song did not really offer much chance for national exposure. While Brooks loved that his work was going to be performed, he still didn't believe he would ever make any money off "Grandma Got Run Over by a Reindeer."

Thanks to Shropshire's inventive mind, however, Brooks would be proven wrong.

Brooks finally got out of Tahoe and back on the road with his band, while Shropshire returned to San Francisco. With a vision for "Grandma," the singer and songwriter — a veterinarian by vocation — formed his own label, bought studio time, and recorded Brooks' unique Christmas ode. The following December, he personally delivered it to San Francisco radio stations, begging disc jockeys to give the song a spin. Soon phone lines lit up with demands to play

Elmo 'n' Patsy's record. Initially it appeared that "Grandma Got Run Over by a Reindeer" was on its way to becoming only a regional hit.

Then the Gray Panthers and local school groups got involved. The Panthers felt the song cast the elderly in a disparaging light. Many teachers and pastors jumped on board, arguing that the concept of a drunken grandparent at Christmas was not a good thing for children. Under mounting pressure, the stations quit playing the song, and local stores refused to stock it.

The song about Grandma should have died right there, but the news stories stirred people's interest, making them want to know what all the fuss was about. With no records to play, radio stations outside of San Francisco obtained bootlegged copies of "Grandma Got Run Over by a Reindeer" from the few outlets that had the single. Within two years, the song had slowly made it across the nation, one radio station at a time.

Shropshire realized that if he had a national record distribution deal, he might have a hit on his hands. He found a partner in Nationwide Sound Distributors in Nashville, Tennessee. Rushing back to San Francisco, the singing vet created a new label. On his Oink imprint, Elmo 'n' Patsy were ready to make their debut on the worldwide stage. To fully assure the exposure the song needed, Shropshire raided his bank account, spending his last thirty thousand dollars to make a music video.

In Shropshire's home, with the help of his friends and family, a wacky Christmas video was shot, with the veterinarian in drag playing the part of the drunken Grandma. The mini-movie's script faithfully followed the song's lyrics until the final verse, when Grandma suddenly fell down the chimney, very much alive.

TNN and MTV were the main video outlets in 1983. Both put the strange novelty Christmas song into heavy rotation. Defying the odds and a host of bad reviews, and thanks to its video, "Grandma Got Run Over by a Reindeer" was the most played Christmas song in the country. As the New Year rolled around, a shocked Brooks had earned his first hit and his band Elmo had made a sleighful of cash.

The single became a perennial holiday visitor for the next fifteen years. As fans' zeal waned, Shropshire reinvigorated the song's popularity through an animated television special. "Grandma" was a hit all over again. By 2008, the song had garnered more than four million unit sales.

The strangest number to top the holiday charts would never have been recorded if not for a snowstorm. Because of that storm, two men met, and "Grandma Got Run Over by a Reindeer" has become one of the top sing-along hits of the holidays. More than three decades after first recording the song, Shropshire is still performing his ode to a hilariously fictional holiday death. Meanwhile, Brooks, who now works in air traffic control at the Dallas – Fort Worth airport, checks his radar every Christmas Eve to make sure no other grandmother wanders into the path of Santa and his reindeer.

ALL I WANT FOR CHRISTMAS IS YOU

*T*hree different songs share the title "All I Want for Christmas Is You," including Mariah Carey's version and a country cut often heard in Louise Mandrell's live shows. The final, which has been recorded by dozens of acts, including Brooklyn Bridge, is, according to many sources such as CBS and *Billboard*, the version most remembered and requested during the holiday season. This "All I Want for Christmas Is You" was created by a unique musician from New Orleans who teamed up with a guitar player to produce a timeless holiday classic.

Andrew John Franichevich Jr. was a baby boomer and embraced fully the perspective of those post–World War II babies. Though he lived in the legendary river city of New Orleans for much of his childhood, the next two decades of Franichevich's life are blanks. From out of nowhere, he seemed to surface as an adult, his name now inexplicably changed to Andy Stone, and he spent time in college until the lure of music drew him from the classroom and onto the stage. Stone then reinvented himself once again as Vince Vance, leader of the Valiants.

In 1970, the Valiants were attracting small crowds with their high-energy stage shows. Often described as a southern rock band, the band couldn't be pigeonholed. Vance's eighteen-inch beehive hair and performance antics mesmerized audiences. People marveled at the group's showmanship as much as at their sound. Most viewed them as too eccentric to land a record contract.

Their showmanship got them a 1971 gig opening for the Allman Brothers, resulting in national exposure. By the time they headlined the Super Dome Mardi Gras Concerts in the midseventies, they were almost always introduced as "the top band in America without a hit record." Vance realized that the hard work and small rewards that went with constant touring paled in comparison with the money made by top recording acts; he also knew that because of his group's eccentric nature, they were viewed by record labels as not viable for radio. In other words, they could make people laugh in concert, but few believed that disc jockeys would play any of their music.

The Valiants continued to labor off the radio radar until Vance came up with a protest song about the 1980 Iran hostage crisis. "Bomb Iran" was set to the tune of the rock-and-roll classic "Barbara Ann" and became a novelty number played from coast to coast. Though the song remained in rotation for weeks, the single didn't chart because it lacked distribution to most record outlets. While Vance and his band gained exposure, they still didn't have a major record deal or a legitimate hit.

In the fall of 1982, the Valiants were involved in a late-night automobile accident that claimed the life of lead guitarist Richard Heath. The surviving members of the band were badly injured, and the group didn't return to the stage for almost six months. Buoyed by a cultlike following of fans, the Valiants continued performing at clubs and music festivals for the next six years. The group seemed to be on its last legs when Vance was presented with a winning idea.

According to a story Vance told to the Associated Press and dozens of local newspapers, in August 1988 the Valiants were scheduled to perform at Pennsylvania's Hershey Park. Vance enlarged his band to include a group of girl singers he called the Valianettes, and his sound ranged from rock to blues to country. Staying in a cheap hotel, sharing a room with his lead guitarist, Troy Powers, Vance and the musician were killing time when Powers said, "I've got the perfect title for a Christmas song: 'All I Want for Christmas Is You.'" Vance laughed, then agreed the hook was a good one.

In suffocating heat, with little else to do, they began the process of creating lyrics about holiday desire. They took the point of view of a lonely soul whose only Christmas wish was for the one person he loved to come and knock at the door. Vance and Powers went back and forth on the direction and pacing of the words. Vance wanted the piece to have a classic feel of heartache and won the struggle for the song's style and tone.

The songwriters set their holiday poetry against a melody line that harkened back to the early 1960s. Bearing a resemblance to the Bobby Vinton hit "My Heart Belongs Only to You," the song had enough new riffs to sound fresh as well as nostalgic. Vance, who wanted the piece to have a timeless air, knew that if his group was going to sing a holiday song, the tune had to be something that could be played in any era and for any age group.

After testing "All I Want for Christmas Is You" in their shows, the Valiants, who still couldn't find a record label willing to take a chance on them, cut the song and created their own label. It was a risky move, since the group was absorbing all the costs and had no promotional or distribution possibilities. Lisa Layne's bluesy voice supplied the lead lines; she didn't so much slide through the lines as attack them. Her vocals pushed the number into something with jazz and blues influence. The smoky, sultry sound crossed every genre but one — country. But ironically, the country music market first picked up on the record.

Without a national distribution deal, the single was limited in publicity and sales. For the next three years, "All I Want for Christmas Is You" struck a chord with only a small number of listeners. Vance needed to jump-start sales. He turned to a medium that was creating a whole new generation of stars: music videos.

In 1993, producer Steve Dunning brought the Valiants into the studio to film a video version of the holiday song. The video captured images of a woman decorating her tree and longing for her sweetheart, with scenes of Vance buying presents. She is yearning for her lover while he is out shopping for the gifts he thinks she wants. The three-and-a-half-minute video was chock-full of typical Christmas scenes of Santa hats, mistletoe, and store displays. It was almost sentimental, until Vance showed up with his trademark hair. Still, even with the unique look of the video's hero, "All I Want for Christmas Is You" came off as whimsical and sweet because of its special message of love being the most important gift of all. When the storyline played out and the lovers were united at the end of the final chorus, the song reflected a classic Hollywood love story.

Though the song received some rotation in all video outlets during Christmas of 1993, CMT and TNN played it the most. A lot of the country genre's fans had grown up as fans of Elvis, Bobby Vinton, and the Platters. This song spoke to them and reminded them of falling in love.

Thanks to the thousands of fan requests and the heavy rotation of the video on cable outlets, Vance secured a national distribution deal and, almost twenty-three years into his career, landed a record on the national playlists. Even he couldn't have predicted the depth of the song's appeal. Over the next decade, the single became a huge holiday hit. In 2008, *Billboard* magazine reported that "All I Want for Christmas Is You" had emerged as the most played country holiday song. As the song's popularity soared, scores of acts cut "All I Want for Christmas Is You," including pop/country sensation Leann Rimes and the popular nostalgia band Brooklyn Bridge.

Vance's holiday song assured him a living for the rest of his life. He performed at the White House and because of this one holiday tune was invited to meet the Pope while the latter was on a U.S. tour. The music video is one of the most popular holiday offerings on the internet, and according to iTunes sales statistics, the online downloads of "All I Want for Christmas Is You" exceed the record sales of the original release.

While Vance's Christmas hit will never be as revered as "White Christmas" or "The Christmas Song," this number has carved out a niche as one of the rare holiday classics that thousands of couples claim as their song. Vance and Powers seemed to understand that all the presents in the world can't wipe out loneliness. The lyrics of "All I Want for Christmas Is You" are much deeper and much more meaningful than even the writers first imagined. The words to this song, which was viewed as just a fun Christmas number, mean so much more because they are not just heard by the ears; they are felt in the heart. It is those emotions that seem to make this unique cut a Christmas classic.

CHRISTMAS SHOES

hristmas hits have traditionally been promoted largely by radio requests. But as the world crossed into a new millennium, that suddenly changed. In 2000, a song was inspired and birthed by the internet — all because of an emailed story. The inspiration for this Christmas song, a modern carol more than twenty years in the making, would have been lost in the plains of the Midwest if not for cyberspace.

On a cold winter day in the late 1970s, Helga Schmidt was trying to complete her Christmas shopping. When Schmidt finished her shopping, she found herself waiting in a long line. Schmidt noticed two children standing in front of her. Leaning closer, Schmidt could see that the girl was holding a pair of women's shoes. The woman smiled, thinking that it was probably a present for their mother or grandmother. As she watched them, she wondered who they were and why she had never seen them before. After all, she knew almost everyone in town.

Schmidt felt as if she had been magically transported into a Norman Rockwell painting. She noted the wonder on the kids' faces, the music playing over a loudspeaker, and the decorations above her head. This idyllic aura continued until the clerk took the shoes and rang them up. The children's smiles disappeared when the clerk announced the price of the shoes.

"Are you sure?" the boy asked.

"Yes," said the exhausted clerk.

Placing all their coins and bills on the counter, the disappointed children looked back at the clerk. She quickly fingered through the small stack of silver and copper coins before announcing, "You're three dollars short."

"This is all we have," the girl announced, tears streaming from her eyes.

"Then you'll have to put the shoes back and buy something else," she said. "Now move along; you're holding up the line."

Schmidt could see that the gift had special meaning to them. They had to have it. But why? Why not a hairbrush or a piece of costume jewelry? What was so important about these particular shoes? She had to know. She reached into her purse and pulled out three dollars. As she handed the clerk the money, the children smiled and politely said, "Thank you so much!"

A few moments later, with the shoes in a sack, the children bounced toward the exit. Stopping at the door, they turned to again look at their benefactor. As their eyes met Schmidt's, they smiled. Rather than rush out, they waited for the woman to pay for her purchases.

As Schmidt approached them, both kids said in unison, "Thanks."

"You are very welcome," the woman answered. "This gift must mean a lot to you."

"The shoes are for our mother," the little girl explained. "She's very sick and is going to heaven real soon."

"These shoes will match the streets of gold in heaven," the boy said. "We learned about those streets in Sunday school class."

The children turned and disappeared into the street.

Schmidt could not shake the image of the children from her head. She wanted to know who they were and where they lived, but no one in the store knew them, and they had gotten away before she could ask.

A few days later, Schmidt's college class was given an assignment to write about a recent experience. She penned the story of the Christmas shoes. Her professor submitted the story to a local church newsletter. The following year, a host of other church publications picked it up. A decade later, it was reprinted in one of the best-selling Chicken Soup books. Then someone posted it as an email forward in the mid-1990s. That one forward became a hundred, then a thousand, and then a million. By 1999, it was one of the most circulated stories online.

During the months leading up to the final holiday of the twentieth century, Eddie Carswell found the story of the Christmas shoes in his inbox. Like millions of others, Carswell couldn't shake the image of the children and their special present purchased for a dying mother. Carswell was a member of the Christian group Newsong. The quintet of Carswell, Matt Butler, Billy Goodwin, Michael O'Brien, and Scotty Wilbanks had placed seventeen number 1 singles on Christmas charts. Their "Arise, My Love," "Red Letter Day," and "People Get Ready" even became crossover hits on mainstream radio. Newsong was the perfect musical vehicle to carry a new song up playlists.

Working with a friend, Leonard Ahlstrom, Carswell created a musical version of Schmidt's story. Newsong recorded and released the number in time for the century's first Christmas season. The timing couldn't have been worse. During this special millennium year, most people seemed to be longing for the traditional songs. Most radio stations were shying away from new material. Newsong might have been popular, but they were not hot enough to break the public's nostalgia. As the holidays approached, "The Christmas Shoes" was left out in the cold.

However, a few stations in Kansas and Nebraska picked up the song. Soon email, generated by those who had heard the tune on rural radio stations or at Newsong's concerts, carried the story of the song around the world, and thanks to the internet, people began calling large-market stations, demanding to hear the story of "The Christmas Shoes." This online movement soon lifted Newsong's holiday release to number 1 on *Billboard*'s adult contemporary chart. The song topped Christian charts and landed on R&B and country playlists.

Because no one had expected much from the new carol, the music industry began to call it "the little song that could." A better description may be "the little song that could not be stopped."

Thanks to the success of the recording, millions again forwarded the original email story. This led to the best-selling novel based on the story and to CBS turning the concept into a movie. The first new holiday hit of the twenty-first century, "The Christmas Shoes" also demonstrated the power of the internet to shape our holiday celebrations.

A decade later, music is promoted online more than through radio. Downloading has become so common that many have forgotten there was a time when people communicated by mail and records were bought at stores. It's ironic that an event in a small, rural department store would be the inspiration for the song that first showed the power of musical promotion via the web. Thanks to a woman's generosity and two kids' desire to find the perfect gift for their mother, the perfect Christmas story was born. This story, wrapped in the music of "The Christmas Shoes," defines not just what Christmas once was but also what it is and always should be. Perhaps that is why a holiday hit has become such a timeless favorite even in the information age.

SILENT NIGHT

"ilent Night" was the first holiday recording to become
a national hit. Amazingly, it continued to chart for a
variety of different artists for more than four decades.
But before we deal with the electronic record making and
record-breaking history of "Silent Night," it behooves us to
examine the unique calamity that led to the carol's creation.

In 1818, Joseph Mohr was a twenty-five-year-old priest
serving at the St. Nicholas Church in Oberndorf, Austria.
Working beneath a veteran priest, the young clergyman
was rarely given what he considered important duties. But
in early fall, Mohr was assigned the task of organizing the
music for the Christmas Eve Mass.

The young priest dove into this job with wild abandon.
He loved music, had a great knowledge of the German and
Austrian carols and of classical pieces as well, and foresaw
a service that combined elaborate organ arrangements with
harmonious choral music. When he wasn't working with
parish children or trying to meet the needs of the local poor,
Mohr gave every spare moment to making his grand plans

for the most elaborate Christmas Eve service in church history a reality.

Mohr knew he faced some challenges for the holiday service. His church was old and the organ was temperamental. The entire area had been struck by one of the coldest periods of winter weather Austria had seen in years. With snow stacked ten feet high, people struggled to keep their homes warm. The local economy had been hit hard by the extreme weather. Members of the choir missed practice because of the icy conditions. As the sun broke through the clouds on Christmas Eve, the priest had seen enough progress to hope for at least moderate success.

A few hours before the service, Mohr made his way down the snow-covered streets of Oberndorf to St. Nicholas Church. After stoking the fire, he lit a candle and kneeled to ask God's blessing on the evening's proceedings. Almost as an afterthought, he sat down at the church organ to play through a few of the carols they would be using that night.

The instrument was dead.

For more than half an hour, Mohr employed every trick he knew to try to get the organ working. He fiddled with keys, stops, and pedals and even crawled behind the console. The organ remained silent, its voice as still as a dark winter's night. With nothing further he could do, the priest collapsed in a state of despair. He was destined to fail at the most important job he had ever been given. Worse yet, the musical part of the service would be a truly silent night.

People in trouble usually seek out friends. Mohr's best

friend was Franz Gruber. Hurrying up the steps to the thirty-one-year-old schoolteacher's drafty apartment, the priest banged on the door. When the teacher answered the insistent knocking, he was shocked to find Father Mohr. The priest should have been at the church preparing for services, not making the rounds visiting old friends. Mohr was no doubt hoping that Gruber, who had once studied organ with noted teacher Georg Hartdobler, might have some idea how to fix the old instrument at St. Nicholas. The schoolteacher didn't have any ideas, but he offered to play his guitar during the service.

The idea of Gruber accompanying the choir with the guitar had merit, but Mohr felt that none of the songs the choir had practiced would work with the instrument. As the two leafed through an old music book, looking for simpler carols, inspiration struck.

A few years earlier, while assigned to a church in Mariapfarr, Mohr had written a Christmas poem. The six unadorned stanzas had been inspired on a winter's walk. For reasons he couldn't explain, Mohr had brought the poem with him when he was transferred to the church in Oberndorf. If he could find it, his friend might be able to compose the music.

Racing home, Mohr searched his modest room. He found "Stille Nacht, Heilige Nacht" in the bottom drawer of his desk.

> *Silent night, holy night!*
> *All is calm, all is bright.*

Round yon Virgin, Mother and Child.
Holy infant so tender and mild,
Sleep in heavenly peace,
Sleep in heavenly peace.

Silent night, holy night!
Shepherds quake at the sight.
Glories stream from heaven afar
Heavenly hosts sing Alleluia,
Christ the Savior is born!
Christ the Savior is born.

Silent night, holy night!
Son of God, love's pure light.
Radiant beams from Thy holy face
With the dawn of redeeming grace,
Jesus Lord, at Thy birth.
Jesus Lord, at Thy birth.

Buoyed by hope, he shoved the worn paper into his coat pocket and fought his way back through the snowy streets to Gruber's.

The song saved Christmas at the little church. But in spite of the congregation's quick acceptance of "Stille Nacht," Mohr's song might have been relegated back to the desk drawer to languish there forever, unknown to those outside of Oberndorf, without the intervention of a third party.

In January, Karl Mauracher, an organ repairman from the Ziller Valley, arrived at St. Nicholas to fix the organ. As he worked, Mohr shared the story of how he had used a guitar and an original composition at the Christmas Eve mass. Mauracher asked the priest to sing the song. The repairman liked "Stille Nacht" so much that he jotted down the words and learned the melody. Mauracher taught the song to churches all over Europe. Within a decade, thousands of choirs were using it at Christmas.

In 1832, the Stasser family sang in a small community where Mauracher was installing an organ. During their stay, this family learned "Stille Nacht." A few weeks later, at a concert in Leipzig, the Stassers performed the carol in front of a large crowd at a fair. One of those attending was King William IV of Prussia. He was so moved by the song that he requested that his nation's Cathedral Choir sing "Stille Nacht" at his annual Christmas celebration. This was the big break the carol needed to become a European hit. Within seven years, the song crossed the Atlantic.

In December 1839, the Austrian family singing group the Rainers traveled to New York. During one of their performances, the family sang "Stille Nacht" in English for a huge crowd at Trinity Church. Thanks to this performance, within a decade the song became America's most popular Christmas carol. Its power was so great that on Christmas Days during the war between the Union and the Confederacy, it was not unusual for hostilities to cease and troops on both sides to be heard singing the holiday classic.

By the late nineteenth century, "Silent Night" had been translated into more than twenty languages and was a vital part of Christmas celebrations all around the world. Like the celebration of Christmas itself, by the start of the twentieth century "Silent Night" had moved out of the church and into the mainstream.

Still, even though everyone was singing the song and it could be found in hymnals and songbooks all around the globe, there was one musical realm it had not yet entered. In 1905, when the immensely popular recording group the Haydn Quartet cut Mohr's eighty-year-old holiday number, the song made another important move that paved the way for the future introduction of Christmas classics. Named for the renowned composer, the quartet was formed in 1896 to record new disks for Thomas Edison's studio. Usually recording *a cappella*, the group, made up of John Bieling, Harry Macdonough, S. H. Dudley, and William F. Hooley, became the standard bearers for the popular barbershop harmonies sweeping the nation at the turn of the century. Macdonough's tenor was the group's driving force and set them apart from other recording quartets of the era. Charting first in 1898, the group had its initial number 1 hit with "Because" in the fall of 1900. A long string of other best sellers followed.

In 1905, the group decided to take a huge risk and cut a holiday record. Seasonal music had not sold well in the past. Still, the Haydn Quartet pushed forward and, in a fall session, recorded their version of Mohr's song. In cutting "Silent Night," the group employed a lyric substitution that is rarely heard today. Rather than singing "silent night, holy night," the Haydn Quartet sang "silent night, hallowed night." For more than a generation, millions would follow this lead and sing the carol with these lyrics.

Released in late fall, the Haydn Quartet's recording first charted in early December, and it raced to number 2 by the holidays. Without radio, the huge sales were spurred by great newspaper reviews and word of mouth.

Three years later, internationally known, German-born opera singer Ernestine Schumann-Heink had the second major hit with "Silent Night." Schumann-Heink's century-old recording is such a dramatic rendition that it has been reissued on CD and is still being played all around the globe in the twenty-first century.

The Neapolitan Trio took "Silent Night" to number 7 in 1917. This would mark the first time the carol became a popular instrumental hit. Eleven years later, Paul Whiteman and His Orchestra took the Austrian holiday classic into the top 10, landing at the sixth spot. This time sales were enhanced by radio exposure.

Whiteman's group numbered more than twenty musicians and included everything from strings to a banjo. They were billed as the world's greatest jazz band, but in truth their focus was on pop music. Though critics often panned their work as little more than commercial jingles with little substance, the public loved Whiteman's style. Thus, the band was one of the most featured groups on radio.

In 1936, radio and movie star Bing Crosby was asked to appear in a short documentary around the holidays to help raise money for a Catholic charity group committed to feeding hungry children in China. A native of Tacoma, Washington, Crosby had left home when he was a teen, working with various bands as a vocalist. After years on the road, he landed a CBS radio contract and became a recording artist for the Brunswick label. He was already becoming a teen sensation when he was discovered by Paramount Pictures in 1930. Using the power of radio and motion pictures, he initiated an unparalleled string of best-selling records. Over the next forty years, he would place more than 350 singles in the top 40. The only American singers who rivaled his success were Frank Sinatra and Elvis Presley.

As a part of his work with the charity, Crosby offered to sing a Christmas song and naturally chose the world's best-known carol. With his crooning baritone, "Silent Night" seemed to be the perfect choice. Crosby didn't plan on cutting a record of the carol. He didn't want to make money from religious music. He relented only when his brother Bob pointed out that Bing could assign all the royalties to the charity group. Little did Bing know that his recording would not only land at number 7 on the *Billboard* charts but also begin a tradition that would see him becoming an iconic voice in holiday music for the next four decades. In the more than thirty years since Bing's passing, his version has remained one of the most played of the traditional carols, and it is still generating funds for charity groups.

Recorded thousands of times by many of the greatest voices in the entertainment world, this simple song, created in a panic to save one small Christmas Eve service, remains the most beloved and highest-selling traditional carol. The composers of "Silent Night," Joseph Mohr and Franz Gruber, didn't live long enough to fully grasp what they had penned. Both died penniless, aware only that their carol was gaining popularity as part of the holiday season in Austria and Germany. The song, which saved Christmas for a congregation at St. Nicholas Church, has become a holiday favorite for hundreds of millions.

Stories behind Christmas Boxed Set

Ace Collins, Bestselling Author

Since angels sang when Jesus was born, music has been as much a part of Christmas as candy canes, Christmas trees, and other beloved traditions of the season. Now you and your family can deepen your celebration of Christ's birth as you learn the stories and spiritual significance of our most cherished holiday songs and traditions.

Do you understand the meaning of "God Rest Ye Merry Gentlemen"? Why do we use red and green at Christmas? What is the origin of the Christmas tree? Do you know the unusual history behind "O Holy Night"?

Written by popular music historian and bestselling author Ace Collins, the three books in this beautiful boxed set unlock the origins and meanings of best-loved carols, hymns, and songs. They also explain traditions as familiar yet little understood as mistletoe, ornaments, stockings, and holly. From the cloisters of fifth-century monks, to the frontlines of World War II, to Hollywood sets and Nashville recording studios, Collins takes you on a journey that will warm your heart and enrich your experience of this brightest of holiday seasons.

Available in stores and online!

ZONDERVAN®
.com

25 Days, 26 Ways to Make This Your Best Christmas Ever

Ace Collins, Bestselling Author

Christmas should be the most anticipated day of the year. But many people
dread the shopping, financial strain, and
extra activities they have to sandwich
between the layers of their already too-busy lives.

Bestselling author Ace Collins is the perfect guide to help
you navigate the stress of the holidays. As he shares twenty-six
easy ways to revamp Christmas expectations, you will relax, re-
fuel, and readjust your attitude toward the season. Each upbeat
chapter contains easy to apply ideas for taking a fresh look at a
holiday tradition or task and making it positive and meaningful.
Through a blend of historical stories, scriptural truths, and contemporary anecdotes, Collins creates a recipe for holiday happiness. He adeptly shows how to keep the joy of the season from
derailing and helps you rediscover Christmas as it was meant to
be — holy, peaceful, and purposeful.

A glorious Christmas is attainable with Collins' timely wis-
dom and advice. Partly devotional, partly practical, and always
thoughtful, Collins' book will help you make this your best
Christmas ever!

Available in stores and online!

Farraday Road

Ace Collins, Bestselling Author

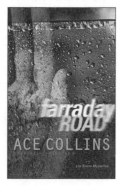

A quiet evening ends in murder on a muddy mountain road.

Local attorney Lije Evans and his beautiful wife, Kaitlyn, are gunned down. But the killers don't expect one of their victims to live. After burying Kaitlyn, Lije is on a mission to find her killer — and solve a mystery that has more twists and turns than an Ozark-mountain back road.

When the trail of evidence goes cold, complicated by the disappearance of the deputy who found Kaitlyn's body at the scene of the crime, Lije is driven to find out why he and his wife were hunted down and left for dead along Farraday Road. He begins his dangerous investigation with no clues and little help from the police. As he struggles to uncover evidence, will he learn the truth before the killers strike again?

Available in stores and online!

ZONDERVAN®
.com

Stories behind the Traditions and Songs of Easter

Ace Collins, Bestselling Author

The treasured traditions of Easter — little bunnies, parades, new Easter outfits, sunrise services, passion plays, and more — infuse our celebration of the season with meaning and glowing memories. And in ways you may not realize, they point us to the resurrection of Christ and our hope of life beyond the grave. *Stories behind the Traditions and Songs of Easter* reveals the events and backgrounds that shaped the best-loved customs and songs of Easter, introducing you to stories you've never heard and a deeper appreciation for the holiday's familiar hallmarks.

Available in stores and online!

Sticks and Stones

Using Your Words as a Positive Force

Ace Collins, Bestselling Author

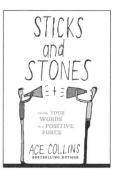

Of the roughly thirty-thousand words you will speak today, imagine if just a handful of them could save a life ... or heal a broken heart ... or inspire a vision that would shape the course of history.

Today is your opportunity to speak — or write — words of incalculable potential for good. With simple action points and colorful stories, this inspiring book will help you weed out sticks-and-stones negativism and unleash the surpassing, life-giving, destiny-shaping power of positive words.

What does it take for your words to make a difference? Perhaps a simple thank-you letter. Maybe an encouraging email. Or a simple hello, a thoughtful phone call, a note written on the back of a family photograph ... the possibilities are endless. *Sticks and Stones* shows you the power and importance of your words, and how to use the right words to have a positive impact beyond anything you can imagine.

Stories Behind the Hymns That Inspire America

Songs That Unite Our Nation

Ace Collins, Author of the best-selling Stories Behind the Best-Loved Songs of Christmas

From the moment the pilgrims landed on the shores of the New World, to the dark days following September 11th, songs of faith have inspired, comforted, and rallied our beloved country. *Stories Behind the Hymns That Inspire America* describes the people, places, and events that have shaped the heart and soul of America. The stories behind these songs will fascinate you and bring new meaning and richness to special spiritual moments in the history of our nation.

The songs in this book have energized movements, illuminated dark paths, commemorated historic events, taken the message of freedom and faith across this nation and beyond, healed broken spirits, and righted wrongs. Their stories will make you proud of your heritage as you realize anew that in America, even one voice can make a lasting influence.

Available in stores and online!

Share Your Thoughts

With the Author: Your comments will be forwarded to
the author when you send them to *zauthor@zondervan.com*.

With Zondervan: Submit your review of this book
by writing to *zreview@zondervan.com*.

Free Online Resources at
www.zondervan.com

Zondervan AuthorTracker: Be notified whenever your favorite
authors publish new books, go on tour, or post an update
about what's happening in their lives at www.zondervan.com/
authortracker.

Daily Bible Verses and Devotions: Enrich your life with daily
Bible verses or devotions that help you start every morning
focused on God. Visit www.zondervan.com/newsletters.

Free Email Publications: Sign up for newsletters on Christian
living, academic resources, church ministry, fiction, children's
resources, and more. Visit www.zondervan.com/newsletters.

Zondervan Bible Search: Find and compare Bible passages in
a variety of translations at www.zondervanbiblesearch.com.

Other Benefits: Register yourself to receive online benefits
like coupons and special offers, or to participate in research.

ZONDERVAN.com/
AUTHORTRACKER
follow your favorite authors